ROUTLEDGE LIBRARY EDITIONS: PHILOSOPHY OF EDUCATION

Volume 2

DO TEACHERS CARE ABOUT TRUTH?

T0347551

DO TEACHERS CARE ABOUT TRUTH?

Epistemological Issues for Education

E. P. BRANDON

Routledge
Taylor & Francis Group

LONDON AND NEW YORK

First published in 1987 by Allen & Unwin (Publishers) Ltd

This edition first published in 2017
by Routledge
2 Park Square, Milton Park, Abingdon, Oxon OX14 4RN

and by Routledge
711 Third Avenue, New York, NY 10017

Routledge is an imprint of the Taylor & Francis Group, an informa business

© 1987 E. P. Brandon

All rights reserved. No part of this book may be reprinted or reproduced or utilised in any form or by any electronic, mechanical, or other means, now known or hereafter invented, including photocopying and recording, or in any information storage or retrieval system, without permission in writing from the publishers.

Trademark notice: Product or corporate names may be trademarks or registered trademarks, and are used only for identification and explanation without intent to infringe.

British Library Cataloguing in Publication Data
A catalogue record for this book is available from the British Library

ISBN: 978-1-138-20902-2 (Set)
ISBN: 978-1-315-45789-5 (Set) (ebk)
ISBN: 978-1-138-69230-5 (Volume 2) (hbk)
ISBN: 978-1-138-69231-2 (Volume 2) (pbk)
ISBN: 978-1-315-53265-3 (Volume 2) (ebk)

Publisher's Note
The publisher has gone to great lengths to ensure the quality of this reprint but points out that some imperfections in the original copies may be apparent.

Disclaimer
The publisher has made every effort to trace copyright holders and would welcome correspondence from those they have been unable to trace.

Preface to the Re-issue

This little book was first published in 1987. What I saw as my task then was to point to issues in philosophy that might be of use to teachers when they faced questions relating to truth and knowledge. While no doubt much has changed in the decades since, I would still think that this is a reasonable way to approach this area of philosophy for education.

The choices I made then were to rely much more on issues in philosophy of science – broadly logical questions of the relations and status of the claims we make – than to talk about the questions of central concern to epistemology or the theory of knowledge generally. One pleasing consequence of that choice is that, if what I said was on the right lines in 1987, it remains so: logic, at least at the simple level I was using, doesn't change much. And I still think that emphasis remains defensible. Epistemology has of course changed considerably – there has been much interest in 'virtue' epistemology, and the whole field has been upended by Timothy Williamson's *Knowledge and Its Limits* (Oxford University Press, 2000) which argued against the almost universally accepted notion that our concept of knowledge could be broken down into other components (often justified true belief plus we-know-not-what to avoid Gettier problems, or some version of non-accidentally true belief) and advocated a 'knowledge first' agenda in which knowledge would remain unanalysed. These and other developments in general epistemology, however fascinating they are for philosophers, have not, so far as I can see, provided much that teachers can exploit either in their teaching or in their own understanding of what it is they teach.

Philosophy of science likewise has not stood still. Popper's light has somewhat dimmed, though A.F. Chalmers' *What Is This Thing Called Science?* has now reached its fourth edition (Open University Press, 2013) and retains its modified Popperian perspective. Its revisions reflect the growth of Bayesian approaches to the dynamics of belief-change, greater attention to the role of experiments and the reproducible phenomena they often exhibit, and a more nuanced and selective approach to questions of realism in the interpretation of scientific theory. I might now say something on each of these, and also on the place of models in our scientific attempts to grasp the world, and I might try to counter the exclusive focus on physics – biology is now much more prominent as a source of ideas and examples – but I don't think these developments undermine anything I said before.

To the extent that many educators hope that what is taught will enhance students' ability to reason correctly and avoid fallacy, Bayesianism and probability theory in general have much to contribute (think of the frequency of base-rate fallacies, for which, and for many other failures to think straight, see Stuart Sutherland, *Irrationality*, Pinter & Martin, 2007). But to take up these issues would shift the book's focus to the promotion of critical thinking, rather than a deeper grasp of the nature of the subject-content that is being taught.

If I were writing it now, what I would stress is something about the tools I used, the distinctions made, the logical and other philosophical notions employed. These were treated too reverentially – I would now offer philosophical insights much more explicitly in the style of bricolage, provisional approaches that may clarify an issue but which are not the last word (see my contribution, 'Philosophy as Bricolage' to *What Philosophy Is*, edited by Havi Carel and David Gamez, Continuum, 2004). This is an extension of Popperian fallibilism to philosophy itself – if any induction is reliable, a pessimistic induction to the supersession of any philosopher's position must be near the top. But just as we continue to use Newtonian conceptions to get us to the moon, although we know they are ultimately inadequate to the nature of things, so I think we can continue to find insight in philosophical notions, such as perhaps the synthetic a priori or the fact/value distinction, while recognising that they have their limitations.

Do Teachers Care About Truth?

Epistemological Issues for Education

E. P. BRANDON

London
ALLEN & UNWIN
Boston   Sydney   Wellington

© E. P. Brandon, 1987
This book is copyright under the Berne convention. No reproduction without
permission. All rights reserved.

Allen & Unwin (Publishers) Ltd,
40 Museum Street, London, WC1A 1 LU, UK

Allen & Unwin (Publishers) Ltd,
Park Lane, Hemel Hempstead, Herts, HP2 4TE, UK

Allen & Unwin, Inc.,
8 Winchester Place, Winchester, Mass. 01890, USA

Allen & Unwin (Australia) Ltd,
8 Napier Street, North Sydney, NSW 2060, Australia

Allen & Unwin NZ Ltd,
60 Cambridge Terrace, Wellington, NZ

First published in 1987

British Library Cataloguing in Publication Data

Brandon, E. P.
    Do teachers care about truth?: epistemological issues for education. —
    (Introductory studies in philosophy of education)
1. Knowledge, Theory of
I. Title   II. Series
121 BD161
ISBN 0-04-370174-4

Library of Congress Cataloging-in-Publication Data

Brandon, E. P.
    Do teachers care about truth?
    (Introductory studies in philosophy of education)
Bibliography: p.
Includes index.
1. Education – Philosophy. 2. Truth. I. Title. II. Series.
LA132.B715   1987   370'.1   86-28714
ISBN 0-04-370174-4

Set in 11 on 12 point Plantin by Fotographics (Bedford) Ltd
and printed in Great Britain by
Billings and Sons Ltd, London and Worcester

Contents

	Preface	xi
1	Introduction	1
2	Truth	8
3	Knowledge	28
4	Opinion	63
	Notes	78
	Further Reading	79
	References	81
	Index	84

Preface

This book attempts to set out some ideas about the nature of our knowledge and to make a few suggestions about what they might mean for teachers. In the context of the series in which it appears, it is intended as a survey of general issues in the theory of knowledge that might have implications for education. This task is made somewhat awkward by the need to explain and defend the claims about truth and knowledge that are made, while still keeping space for their possible pedagogical implications. Since I think the main implication concerns getting the status of our knowledge right, I have devoted most of my space to trying to explain the philosophical issues. But of course a great deal has had to be left unsaid or undefended. The theory of knowledge and its specialities such as the philosophy of science are extremely large areas of philosophical inquiry. I have had to choose topics that seem to me to be relevant to at least some teachers, but many of their questions will here go unanswered.

The book owes its existence to the kindness of various people. I would like to single out John Gingell, Phil Snelders, the staff at Allen & Unwin and my Head of Department, Marlene Hamilton, whose zeal for moving us into the twentieth century produced the word-processing facilities without which this volume would never have been finished. Its contents have benefited from the comments of Zellynne Jennings, Jacquie Moriah and Graham Webb.

The philosophical position sketched here derives in large part from the teaching and writings of the late John Mackie. But he not only influenced my philosophical views; he also exemplified that passion for truth which underlies the view of education taken here. In this connection, I should also like to invoke the memory of two other men who, in very different ways, were fired with the same passion: Don Carter and Bryan Matthias. To write of education one must have met educators; I am privileged to have known these teachers.

1

Introduction

Praestat opes sapientia[1]

Education and Truth

The question I have chosen to answer is 'Do teachers care about truth?' Many of you might well react to such a question by saying that it is not worth asking: of course teachers care about truth! All of us do, at least most of the time. We don't set out to mislead other people or lie to them. And when teachers are teaching they will probably be particularly scrupulous. They would emphatically reject what they saw as the teaching of falsehood, error or misunderstanding. And so you might say it is obvious that they do care about truth.

My supposition that many of you would react in this way can in fact be given a good measure of empirical support. Julian Haes (1982) recently asked a group of teachers whether it was important for curriculum content to be true and he found that 'there is a consistently maintained view . . . that, though not necessarily clearly defined, truth is in some way important for the curriculum' (p. 69). The quotations he gives exemplify both the general belief that truth matters and the difficulties teachers have with the notions of truth and knowledge. I hope our later discussions will help you to find a path through these difficulties. For now I just want to say that the issues we consider should also show you why I think my question is worth asking and why the educational establishment may not come out of the examination as well as might be hoped.

Before illustrating some of the fundamental problems that arise when we start to think about truth and knowledge, let me also admit that it is not only ordinary teachers who profess a concern for truth

1

but also educational theorists and others who pronounce on the aims of education. To take one of the most widely known, it is crucial for Hirst's (1974) account of a liberal education that what people are initiated into should be the different forms of knowledge we have come to recognize. Hirst's reasons for thinking that his forms are forms of knowledge and not something else are none too clear, but it is obvious that this supposed status gives them a much easier entrée into the curriculum than they might otherwise have. And it is precisely a lingering doubt about the status of religion as knowledge that has made him hesitant about its place in the curriculum (1974, ch. 12).

While Hirst may be taken as representative of the erstwhile liberal consensus on education, radical reformers and de-schoolers are equally concerned that people acquire knowledge and grasp the truth. Though Illich (1971), for instance, puts great stress on the acquiring of skills, his learning webs would also facilitate less practical learning; the crucial thing is that people learn what matters to them and what they can use in their struggles to liberate themselves. Similarly it is no accident that Freire's advice to agricultural extension workers is largely an exposition of a theory of knowledge (1974, esp. pp. 119–27). Nor is it only self-confessed educationalists who put a premium on truth: Finnis, a philosopher with special interests in morality and law, has recently tried to argue for the classical Aristotelian view that 'truth and the knowledge of it is a good objectively worthy of human pursuit' (1977, p. 250).

Educators honour truth and knowledge, but in their more sublime moments they are likely to talk of understanding, rationality, or even wisdom. But it is arguable that these goals centrally involve truth and knowledge. Peters (1981) at least has asserted that 'to be rational is to care about truth' (p. 75).

While understanding may be mainly a matter of putting things into a wider framework, seeing the way they connect with other things, we are surely concerned that this wider context of belief be true, or, at least, the best supported we can currently find. Once we recognize that the general schema we are using to grasp something is false, we can no longer claim a proper understanding, however illuminating our false beliefs may have been. Similarly, I would have thought, wisdom flourishes with true beliefs rather than false ones, although it is by no means clear what exactly wisdom involves.

Rationality is perhaps somewhat clearer; it is certainly a current favourite as an educational aim. But there are certain difficulties with rationality which make it necessary for us to dig a little deeper. Many people find it easier to deal with rationality by deliberately restricting it to the context of choosing a means to a given end. In this context, rational choice is a matter of choosing the means that maximizes, or at least satisfies as well as available alternatives, one's values in the light of one's beliefs about how the world works. Given an end, given beliefs about the world's working, and given a set of values that associate pluses and minuses with various outcomes, rationality becomes simply a matter of choosing consistently. One problem with this deliberately simplified conception is that it does not require us to question the truth of the beliefs about the world, nor the sensibleness of the values or the end to be pursued. But at least given all these, it yields a fairly straightforward answer. Many critics, however, want a stronger conception of rationality that does entail an assessment of the truth of empirical beliefs and the acceptability of the values involved.

One way of moving in that direction without abandoning the clarity of the simplified conception is to note that ends do not exist all on their own; rather they are woven together in a very complicated pattern. One consequence is that crazy ends will very often impinge disastrously on other more sensible ends that a person may have. What is an end for one problem can be criticized in its turn as part of the means for another end (and not necessarily some more general end). In a similar way, false beliefs about the way the world works are in some cases likely to frustrate one's pursuit of a goal. Maximizing one's values on more occasions will then depend on correcting such false beliefs and on revising the more crazy aims. So, at least to some extent, we can say that rationality can only be promoted if we do attend to such critical tasks and, in particular for our present purposes, to the correction of a person's false beliefs about the world. Simple, isolated rationality is too easy; what matters for education is *more* rationality and the greater overall satisfaction it may bring. And so once again we can find a central place for truth and knowledge underneath the educator's explicit concern for rationality.

I have suggested so far that teachers, educational theorists and ordinary people do give truth and knowledge a central place in their thinking about education. And whatever relations schools may have to education, it is true that much of what goes on in them is the inculcation of varied kinds of knowledge, or of what passes for it.

Problems with Truth

Teachers have many problems, but it might seem that worries about the nature of truth or knowledge are not among them. Curiosity may be innate, but it is not given to many of us to wonder whether some of the answers we are given are more reliable than others, or to puzzle over what is involved in something being true. We may ask questions but on the whole we are avid swallowers of answers; the habit of sorting out better from worse answers and of wondering what makes a good answer has not marked a large part of human history, even in literate societies. It is probably less common than we like to imagine even in our own practice.

Even so, teachers do sometimes have to face questions about truth and knowledge because in our societies the problematic nature of at least some sorts of belief is widely recognized. It is easy to come upon serious difficulties once we begin to reflect on curricular realities. In our everyday thinking we are familiar with the distinction between what a person really does know and what he only thinks he knows. This is not an obscure, philosophically motivated distinction but rather part of our ordinary conceptual resources. But what happens when we look at curricula in these terms? Anyone aware of the history of the subjects they teach will know that much of the 'knowledge' taught in 1900, not to mention 1100, would hardly be accepted nowadays. And since there is nothing cognitively special about the present moment, this reflection must give pause to anyone who believes what one of Haes' teachers claimed: 'we shouldn't disseminate something which has to be corrected later or admitted to be false' (Haes, 1982, p. 70). Nor, of course, is it only at other times that our 'knowledge' is different. Different groups both in our own societies and in others hold incompatible views about a vast variety of factual matters, from the intelligibility of classical mathematics to the existence of angels, not to mention differences on evaluative issues. As another of Haes' teachers wrote, 'what may be "true" in one country may not be regarded as true in another' (p. 69).

Another everyday distinction which can cause problems when we apply it to the curriculum is that between factual matters and matters of opinion or of taste. The thoughts that cockroaches lay a lot of eggs and that cockroaches are repulsive are both expressed in grammatically the same sort of sentence (what we shall later call 'indicative' sentences); both invite assessment in terms of truth or falsity; but many of us would be inclined to say that while the first is simply either true or false the second expresses something that is really only a matter of opinion – although in this case an opinion that is widely shared. With this distinction in our hands, what becomes of the literature taught in school or of the moral and social values promulgated in civics or 'family life education'? Of course, some will not accept these applications of the distinction, but they can probably point to other cases of curricular material they would wish to relegate to the opinion side of the fence.

Aesthetic and moral values are one area widely regarded as matters of opinion. But many people also consider religious beliefs similarly as not to be taught as knowledge. Here talk of taste or opinion may yield to talk of faith, but the message for the schools is the same: don't teach these things as straightforward truths such as you find in maths or elementary geography. And this attitude can carry over into scientific or historical theorizing, especially when it abuts on matters dealt with in religion. So evolutionary theory in biology or Marxist theorizing in history or sociology may be regarded as more a matter for individual choice than the structure of DNA or the historical origin of windmills.

These two familiar distinctions, real knowledge versus merely supposed knowledge and real knowledge versus mere opinion, can easily undermine one's confidence in the centrality of truth for education when they are turned on the actual contents of the curriculum. It is tempting, at this stage, to retreat hastily to some form of relativism: to say we teach what we, or the dominant social group in our society, currently hold to be the truth and that is all we can do, that is all there is to truth. Or if we are more impressed by the examples of opinion, we may begin to talk of some things being true for me while others are true for you or for them.

This is a temptation that many fall for. We shall see some of its technical problems in the next chapter, but for now it is important to see that such moves take a great deal of the force away from the educational commitments we looked at earlier. If there is nothing more to truth than social endorsement, how can we save any notion of there having been cognitive progress? Put another way, what cognitively good reasons can we give for preferring our present society's version of things? Of course, there can be a prudential reason – if you started invoking Zeus or phlogiston, you would certainly fail your exams and might even find yourself in an asylum – but few relativists are so hard-bitten as not to want a more pertinent reason for belief in today's theories. Again, if one falls for the 'true for you, not true for me' line it is very difficult to preserve a usable distinction between getting things right and getting them wrong; how are mistakes possible if all we can claim is that things are or are not true for individuals? The educational commitment to truth and knowledge is a selective commitment (perhaps any commitment must be selective), but these kinds of relativism seem likely to let everything through. Relativized truth or knowledge seems unable to issue any non-arbitrary exclusions, and so it gives us no guidance about what education should be seeking to achieve.

So far I have been trying to sketch some of the main general problems about truth and knowledge that might occur to any reflective teacher. But within more specialized areas there are plenty of questions that raise awkward issues about knowledge of the kind that philosophical inquiry ought to be able to address. How does 'guided discovery' relate to the real work of scientists? What can sensibly go on under the rubric of 'integration' and how does it relate to more traditional 'subjects'? What is at stake in correcting such things as spelling or grammar? What stand should one take in the recent disputes between 'positivist' and 'humanist' geographers? I cannot hope to address, let alone answer, these more specialized questions here, but this book is intended to offer a framework in which to think about such problems. We shall look directly at the general problems I have mentioned and that, I hope, will give you tools to move on to any of the more detailed questions that interest you.

Plan of Attack

Part of the difficulty in facing these kinds of question is that people are often unwilling to do here what they do elsewhere: to tidy up and distinguish issues and recognize the need for a modicum of technical terminology or at least the regimentation of everyday expressions. It seems to be assumed that the most profound philosophical problems can continue to be fruitfully discussed without any real attention to the discipline of philosophy; so at least it would appear in the training of most teachers, since the philosophy of education (at least in English-speaking countries recently) has been largely concerned with charting out its own peculiar area rather than applying the lessons of the rest of philosophy to problems faced by teachers. I do not think this attitude can be sustained. Clarification of the general questions about truth and knowledge we have raised requires that we make distinctions, and insist on such distinctions, rather than attempt to carry on with the imprecisions of everyday discussion.

In the rest of this book I shall begin by trying to clear up and dispose of the issue of truth. I say 'dispose of' deliberately since I shall be arguing that the real problems of truth are problems raised by the things that are true, whether or not we try to start pontificating about truth in the abstract. When we look at these things in more detail we shall first see how the attempt to uncover explanations leads to the revision and replacement of a lot of our common sense. Schools in general underplay this breach with ordinary everyday beliefs. We shall also see why at least most of what we consider knowledge is logically provisional so that we cannot help passing on things that may well be revised or rejected later. Here too schools, whether deliberately or not, pass on untenable views about the nature of knowledge. We shall also look at some of the limitations we inevitably face in our attempts to understand the world so that we can see what we can and – perhaps as importantly – cannot expect of our knowledge. Then in the final chapter we shall look at the way our values are intertwined with our other conceptions and how this makes questions of truth or falsehood in many important areas somewhat complicated. At the very end I shall return to our initial question and try to draw the main morals that have arisen from our investigations.

2

Truth

On a huge hill,
Cragged, and steep, Truth stands, and hee that will
Reach her, about must, and about must goe[2]

John Donne's claim applies most forcefully to our halting attempts to reveal the truth, to seek after knowledge; but it applies also to my procedure in this chapter. Before we can say clearly what truth is, we must make several preliminary points.

The Links between Truth and Knowledge

In the previous chapter I continually joined truth and knowledge together in a way that should hardly have caused any surprise. They are different concepts but in the context of educational debate they point us in the same direction. On the one hand, any truths that education is concerned with will be items that don't just turn out to be true by good fortune, but rather items for which teachers or others can produce some defensible reasons to accept as true, which is to say items that are more or less certainly known to be true, though perhaps only to a small group. The truths education deals with are then items of knowledge. On the other hand, anything that really is an item of knowledge is *ipso facto* true. If it is false that Walter Rodney was murdered then no one can know that he was murdered, however vehemently they may believe it. So if anyone

8

says he knows that Rodney was murdered then he is committed to its being true that Rodney was murdered; and if you say of John that he knows Rodney was murdered then you also are committed to its being true that he was.

One problem with these last remarks is that strictly speaking they are not true! You can find competent English speakers saying things like 'The ancient Greeks knew that Zeus lived on Mount Olympus' without themselves endorsing any beliefs about Zeus. If philosophy were simply reduced to recording what people do with their language we would have a very hard time of it. While we need not trouble ourselves with an exact account of what is going on here, I hope it is clear to you that this kind of usage, often called an inverted commas usage from the way it would normally be written, and indeed was written by me in the previous chapter, is secondary or parasitic. It is a way of making a point that could be more straightforwardly made by saying that the ancient Greeks thought they knew that Zeus lived on Olympus, but they were wrong. There is a clear sense in which it is false to say they knew; they only believed. It is false to say they knew because it is false that Zeus lives or lived on Mount Olympus.

We have already seen in the last chapter this distinction between what someone really knows and what they only think they know. It might be worth noting now that it does not just apply to other people. In general we do not in fact know all that we claim to know. And this is one of the facts about ourselves that we can come to know. But there is nothing paradoxical in this – there is no fact that we know and that we don't know at the same time – since in knowing that there are some things we falsely claim to know we do not know which things they may be.

Abbreviations

Before moving on to our next preliminary point, I want to introduce some abbreviations. So far I have been talking about someone knowing something, but this sort of idiom is not very convenient if one wants to talk about the somethings that are known. I shall therefore make a few borrowings from logic and linguistics to let the discussion flow more freely. First of all I want something that can stand for any indicative sentence (we shall look more closely at what an indicative sentence might be in a short time) and I shall use little italic letters starting with p. So if I write 'John knows that p' you can replace the p with something like '$2 + 3 = 5$' or 'Mary loves Tom' or any indicative sentence you like. Such ps and qs function in fact just like the names 'John' or 'Mary' in those examples, since I am not thinking of any particular people; I could equally well have replaced the names with letters and said 'A loves B'; but Mary and Tom make it sound more homely and make it look less like algebra. But if you can see that in saying 'If John knows that p, then p' I am not making a special point about someone called John, but a general claim about knowing something, then I think you should see the point of the ps and qs. If I shall ever want to abbreviate names of people, places or things I shall do as I have just done and use italic capital letters. Besides whole sentences and simple names it will also prove useful to be able to abbreviate two types of phrase, noun phrases (the Queen of England; the way to boil an egg; ...) and verbal phrases (boil an egg; sing sweetly; ...). I shall use NP for noun phrases, VP for verb phrases.

Truth and Being True

We can now move on to our second preliminary point about truth. Philosophical questions are often framed in terms of abstract nouns such as 'truth' or 'justice'. Such abstract nouns give us a way of raising general questions about properties or relations. If someone says that this is a spaniel but that isn't, and we want to ask what is involved in being a spaniel, we are not likely to inquire 'What is spanielhood?', rather we would ask 'What are spaniels like?'; but if someone says that this social set-up is just but that isn't, and we want to ask what is involved in being just, the obvious question the language offers us is 'What is justice?' This would not be a problem but for the fact that people are easily misled into thinking that nouns, even abstract ones, must somehow behave like proper names. And since justice or truth are not concrete things of the sort we meet with in everyday life, there is a tendency to suppose that they must be things we meet with in some extraordinary sphere. Put baldly like that, such an error might seem unlikely but it is safer not to let the danger arise. So we should ask, not 'What is truth?', but 'What is it for something to be true?'

10

Putting it grammatically, we transform the nominalization, 'truth', back into the simple verbal phrase, 'is true'. The philosophical claim underlying this move is that the nominalization is simply a way of talking generally about whatever is conveyed by the simple verbal phrase; there are no other weird entities to be considered.

What Things Are True?

There is yet a third preliminary point before we try to say what is involved in being true. That is to decide which uses of the word we are really interested in. The word 'true' is used in a variety of ways. What someone says can be true, or false, but so can a friend or a horizon. The use I am interested in is, however, the first of those mentioned rather than the others. When we are able to specify what someone has said or believes or hopes or imagines or whatever, we can paraphrase our talk of truth by saying 'It is true that *p*.' It is this use of 'is true' that I am concentrating on.

We need a way of talking about the things that people could say or imagine, about possible contents of thought. I shall use the word 'proposition' to talk about such possible contents of what is said, thought or believed. One very important thing to notice about thinking or believing or the other activities I have alluded to is that if we want to report what is going on we have to use sentences (our *p*s and *q*s) to do it. While you can say things like 'Green!' or 'How ghastly!', if we want to report what you are thinking we would have to say something like 'You think that the green wallpaper clashes horribly with the sofa'. And notice that what comes after the 'think that' could stand on its own as a sentence. My claim is that the same goes for every case in which people think or believe something: thinking or believing is always thinking or believing that *p*, to use the abbreviation we introduced a while ago.

I have said that propositions are always going to require sentences to express them. But only some kinds of sentence can do the job. 'How ghastly the wallpaper is!' is a perfectly good English sentence, as is 'Will you please pass a cucumber sandwich?', but neither of them could report the content of a person's belief. To do that, we need what are often called 'indicative' sentences, not exclamations or questions or imperatives or optatives. The test or criterion I would offer you for indicative sentences (from Hodges,

1977) emphasizes the link between propositions and truth. The test is: can you grammatically enclose your sentence with 'Is it true that . . . ?'? If you can, it is an indicative sentence; if you can't, it isn't. (If it isn't, there are often ways of converting it into indicative form –'The wallpaper is ghastly'; 'You are requested to pass a cucumber sandwich' – but we need not worry about this now.)

I have used both sentences and propositions because there are many occasions when we find that the same sentence can be used, sometimes to say something true, sometimes to say something false; but I want propositions to be true once and for all. If we count sentences in an obvious way, the sentence 'It is raining' can be used one day to say something true (that at 1.30 p.m. on 3 March 1984 it was raining at Mona, Jamaica) and another day (such as 31 January 1985 at 3.30 p.m. at Mona) to say something false. One way to deal with this familiar situation is to say that 'It is raining' is one sentence type which has very many instances or tokens; each time the sentence is used someone produces a sentence token of that type; and each token could be used to make a different statement or, in the terms I am using, to express a different proposition. To talk both of sentences and propositions allows us to count sentences by types and proposition by tokens. This may sound somewhat confusing, but it is really something we all know in our bones; anyway I shall rely on your mastery of the language to allow you to make any similar adjustments to the sentences used to express propositions.

Some Things That Are Not True

More important for our own purposes than the intricacies of propositions and sentences is to be clear about the simple fact that propositions are expressed by complete sentences not just by bits of sentences. When people talk of concepts they are usually thinking of items that would be reflected in language by words or phrases, not by whole sentences. A person may be said to have a concept of a horse, or of equality, but not so felicitously a concept that all men are created equal. A person's use of a concept will be reflected in large part by how he uses 'horse', 'unicorn', 'fraternity', and kindred words. Very roughly, then, we can tie concepts to parts of a sentence, propositions to the whole sentence. What my earlier claim now amounts to is that there is no sense in which concepts can be true or false, since concepts are not themselves propositions.

It is important to see that concepts cannot be true or false. But we should explain why many people have mistakenly thought that they are. In the first place they may have been confusing a proposition's being true with a concept's applying to something. The concept, horse, applies, to something, the concept, unicorn, does not; which is to say, there are horses but there are no unicorns. Take any concept, F, when the proposition that there are Fs is true the concept, F, applies to something; so there is a close link between truth here and the applicability of a concept; but they are not quite the same notions, and it is better to keep them distinct. In the second place, we have to admit that language is very flexible and that what is said in one way can often be said in what is logically a very different way. In the present case, a concept can subsume a proposition or a set of propositions: to talk of the concept of human equality may not be very different from talking of the proposition that all men are created equal, and the concept of evolution usually subsumes for us a complex theory. While this is so, clarity is served by attending to logical niceties, and so we shall continue to insist that concepts are not the sort of things to be true or false.

In this book we must leave aside most of the complex problems that arise in the theory of meaning, but it might be worth making one remark here. People often think of the meaning of their words as fairly precise and specific – the sort of thing they could produce as a 'definition' if requested. Such accounts will often make explicit mention of currently accepted theory – educators, for instance, have a penchant for talking of learning in terms of behaviourist psychology. Now if the meaning of such terms were tied to theories in this way, the meaning of words would change as theories change, and it might be difficult to see how people using different theories were still talking about the 'same things'. One plausible response to this problem is to suggest that many of our concepts are not so specific; putting it in terms of words, one might say that the word 'gold' means whatever it is that underlies features such as the malleability, colour, chemical behaviour, and so on that we associate with the substance we call 'gold'. Such an agnostic rendering of the meaning of a term leaves plenty of room for alternative theories and for alternative ways of putting features together (so some observable features might end up being attributed to impurities in actual specimens rather than to the substance itself) while allowing us to say that these different views are all attempts to delineate the same objective reality. Such less specific accounts of the meaning of terms also square rather better with the diversity of the existing usage of the words associated with particular concepts – it is all too easy to offer an account of a concept while thinking only of a very restricted range of linguistic usage.

Just as I have been insistent that constituents of sentences cannot be true or false, so I want to insist that one kind of structure made up of sentences cannot be true or false either. And that is an argument. An argument is a sequence of sentences (or propositions), some of them making up the premisses of the argument, some of them (usually just one) being the conclusion. For a sequence to be an argument, the premisses must be intended to support the conclusion in some way. We can regiment an argument into a structure like this: $p, q, \ldots$ so r. (Here p and q stand for premisses, and r for the conclusion.) The kind or degree of support given by the premisses to the conclusion can vary. The strongest kind, found in deductive arguments, gives a guarantee that if the premisses are true, the conclusion will be true as well. When an argument actually gives the kind of support its user claims to provide, I shall say that it is a valid argument. (Many people restrict this term to deductive arguments.)

One of the first things a student of logic has to learn is that there is a difference between the validity of an argument and the truth or falsehood of its constituent statements, i.e. its premisses and conclusion, even though one explains validity in terms of the truth, or likely truth, of the conclusion being conditional upon that of the premisses. There may be valid deductive arguments with false premisses and false conclusions; there may be invalid deductive arguments with true premisses and true conclusions. The actual truth or falsehood of the constituents of a deductive argument is in general irrelevant to its validity; what matters is the possibility of certain combinations of truth and falsehood. Of course, if the premisses are known to be true and the conclusion to be false, that suffices to show the argument to be deductively invalid; but in most cases we do not have this knowledge. So in these cases we must be sensitive to the difference between truth and deductive validity. At the moment my only concern is to stress that difference, and the linguistic stipulation that goes along with it, to the effect that we cannot give a sense to arguments being true or false (arguments can be valid or invalid) nor can we interpret the claim that a statement or proposition is valid or invalid (they are true or false).

Simple Truth

Having gone about and about through these various preliminary matters, we are now in a position to say what it is for a proposition to be true, to offer an analysis of truth. Philosophical analyses can include several different things, so I shall indicate what I think I am offering you at the moment. It is intended to be an account of what we are trying to convey when we say that a proposition (or, more colloquially, what someone said, or someone's belief) is true. It should be another, rather longer and more explicit, way of saying the same thing. It is not an attempt to explain how we can legitimately mean what we mean, nor is it an account of what we should be trying to say, nor does it tell us how we can know that what we mean is so. It does not try to raise or answer doubts about what we mean; it simply sets out to report what we do mean.

To adapt one of Mackie's formulations (1973, p. 50), the view I am endorsing is that to say that a proposition is true is to say that things are as they are stated to be in the proposition. If I say that Parkinson's Law is true I am saying that things are as Parkinson's Law says they are. If I say that Nixon's public statements were false I am saying that things were not as Nixon's public statements said they were. If I say that 'Roseau is the capital of Dominica' is true I am saying that things are as 'Roseau is the capital of Dominica' says they are, viz. Roseau is the capital of Dominica. For accuracy's sake, it is worth noting that I am not, however, directly saying that Roseau is the capital of Dominica; my remark is saying something directly about a statement or proposition, that it is true, not about Roseau or Dominica; but given what I do say about that statement you can infer my commitment to the simple claim about Roseau as well.

Mackie called his account a 'simple' theory of truth, and I hope you can agree with him. It may well seem a startlingly unsurprising account to be given after so many pages of preparation. It is simple, but as we proceed I hope you will see that it isn't trivial. Mackie's other label for his account is a 'comparison' theory, since the fundamental point about truth is that it involves a comparison between how things are and how they are said, or believed, or imagined, etc., to be.

One Truth

The word 'truth' is potentially ambiguous (this is another reason for our preference for looking at 'is true'). It can refer to things that are true, propositions as we have decided to call them. So we can say that there are only four truths in the whole of a book, or we can distinguish the truths of chemistry from those of history. On the other hand, 'truth' can be used as we have been using it to talk of the relation between how things are and how they are said to be. I have just given the account I accept of what that relation is like. And in this sense, I think there is only one relation to be accounted for. But people sometimes talk about different kinds of truth in ways that suggest that they might be thinking that there are different kinds of relation, not just different sorts of true proposition. (For a few writers who can reasonably be interpreted in this way, see Waismann, 1953, Hirst, 1974, ch. 6, or, for a non-philosopher, Hillery, 1984.)

It is logically possible that a word like 'true' could cover two or more distinct relations. The term 'sibling' could be said to cover biologically distinct relations such as identical twins, 'ordinary' brothers or sisters, half-brothers or sisters, and possibly others. So it is possible that what is involved in p being true is different from what is involved in q being true. It is possible; but I do not think it is actual, at least in unpremeditated language use. I think that when people use language unself-consciously 'true' means what I have set out above. But sometimes people tell us that what they mean by truth in mathematics or in religion or in literature is different from what it means elsewhere; and perhaps they consistently use the word in their idiosyncratic way. But if they do, I think we can say that they are in danger of confusing themselves and the rest of us, because they are in each case talking about a distinct property or relation which should be given its own name. This is especially so when the other relation lacks the essential comparative content of simple truth. Thus in mathematics, some people will say that truth is a matter simply of being deducible from a set of axioms (e.g. Hirst and Peters, 1970, p. 63). That is an important property, but it is clearly distinct from truth (and can be shown to be distinct even in mathematics by Gödel's theorems) and no good purpose is served by conflating the two.

Simple Truth and Complex Meaning

We can, however, see why some people are inclined to think there are different sorts of truth. (While I shall look at some reasons for making an honest mistake here it is possible that in some educational debate the confusion is more a matter of evading difficult issues such as the nature of mathematical truth or the justification for teaching certain subjects such as literature or religion.) When we say that p is true, we are saying that things are as p says they are. But what this amounts to depends, of course, on exactly what p is saying, on what it means. When, as often happens, that is complex, it may not be an easy matter to answer the question 'Is p true?' A good deal of this complexity is pretty obvious: 'Clive Lloyd is standing still' is a lot simpler than 'Clive Lloyd is l.b.w.', which involves an appeal to a set of rules; 'The Jones family has three children' is simpler than 'The average family has two point two children.' But there are cases in which the complexity may not be so apparent, and in which philosophical doubts can lead to a 'Yes and No' type answer to the question of truth.

Consider two plausible claims: 'Daffodils are yellow' and 'Socrates died courageously.' In the case of the daffodils, I think it is also plausible to claim that what we intend to convey is that daffodils are intrinsically yellow; the property as we see it in normal light is an inherent feature of them. If this is part of what we usually mean, then we are mistaken; there is no such intrinsic property (though there are, of course, various complex intrinsic properties that bear some relation to what is seen in normal light). But in that case, is the original claim true? At one level, it obviously is: daffodils are not red or purple. But in so far as part of what is being said is that they have an intrinsic yellow-as-it-is-perceived, then the claim is in error, as in this pervasive way are most claims about the colours of things. In the case of Socrates, to do something courageously requires certain things to be true of the action (if he had simply died in his sleep it would hardly have been a courageous death), and we can agree that those things did hold of Socrates. But I think we intend rather more than this in talking of courage; the action is held up for admiration, we should take this attitude rather than that towards it. But its being admirable is something over and above its having the required properties and relations for a courageous death; is it also a fact about Socrates' death? If, as I shall later argue that one should, one says that it isn't, one has the same two-part reply to the question of truth. And even if one says that it is a fact, one has still to acknowledge the complexity hidden within the simple term 'courageously'.

Both these examples are controversial, as almost any example in philosophy will be, but if they are allowed they may suggest that our ordinary statements of the truth may not be 'nothing but the truth'. They may on the contrary involve claims, or at least a set of assumptions, that are to be rejected. Our language has not been fashioned for the purpose of telling the plain unvarnished truth, but it is the only language we have, and in judging some of the things we say by using it we have to make allowances for its inaccuracies. To put the matter another way, I think we can say that every indicative sentence offers itself as making a true or false claim (that is the meaning of the linguistic structure, indicative sentence) but that philosophical analysis often reveals that what is really going on is either something different from making true or false claims or, as in the two cases cited above, a conflation of different claims, some of which are acceptable while others may not be. Here, of course, philosophical analysis is not only reporting what we intend to convey; it is describing what is really going on when we use the language.

As a matter of simple logic, if you conjoin two claims, one of which is false, your combined claim is false. So strictly speaking, in the cases cited all such claims are false. But we normally treat them rather as we do claims about mythological beings: Zeus lived on Olympus, not Mount Ararat, though we know that strictly speaking both claims are false because there is no such being as Zeus to live anywhere.

(The other possibility I have just mentioned, where we are not really making true or false claims although we are using indicative sentences, is also controversial, but to see the sort of analyses that have been offered, consider the two indicative sentences: 'I promise to pay you five dollars' and 'If Mabel is a peeress, she is not allowed to vote.' In the first example, some philosophers have wanted to say that the sentence does not make a true or false statement; it is simply the performance of an action. In the second example, other philosophers have wanted to say that what is really going on in 'if p, then q' sentences is 'suppose p, then q', which is a rather more involved matter of asserting q within the supposition that p. We cannot go into the merits of these proposals here, but they perhaps serve to indicate further possibilities in which questions of whether a claim is true or false become rather involved, although truth itself remains as simple as ever.)

Before we move on from the explanation of why people have thought there are different kinds of truth, one last set of points should be made. I have said what it is for a proposition to be true. I have not said what is involved in a proposition being verified, i.e. being shown to be true, nor in its being proved, nor in its being certain. These are all somewhat more complex notions than the notion of truth that I have described, and it is clear that what is involved in verifying or proving one sort of proposition may be very different from what is involved in verifying or proving some other proposition. Truth is too simple for some people; they are more interested in questions of verification, or degrees of certainty, but they are inclined to stretch the notion of truth to include these more complex concerns. If they do so, and if these other matters do differ among different kinds of proposition, then they will find it natural to think in terms of different kinds of truth. But my point now is that truth is distinct from these other notions and that we should not confuse them. It may be true that I drank Yquem on New Year's Day, 1978, although there is no way now of verifying or falsifying that claim, nor any way, indeed any clear sense, in which it could be proved; and obviously no one need be at all sure of it for it still to be true. However important these other notions are, they are not the same notion as truth; and it is truth we are currently dealing with.

Perhaps in passing we should also note that truth is not the same as universal agreement. People may all agree on something, even on the truth of some proposition, without that proposition being true. Of course if you do decide to let 'true' mean what a group of people agree upon then your kinds of truth multiply and conflict with one another. But there is no reason to choose that meaning.

19

Absolute Truth

I have been trying to say what we mean by the notion of truth. Truth is a matter of comparison between how things are and how they are said or imagined to be. I have suggested that this is the only notion of truth that we have. It is not, however, a notion that some people find easy to accept. It is an ambitious notion. It claims an external standpoint from which to judge our thinking. Here we are, with various thoughts or beliefs; there the world is; and the notion of truth seeks to say how it is between these two. Either our thinking has captured something of how the world is or it hasn't. Truth goes beyond our thinking and judges it. Judgements that something is or is not true are not judgements from one perspective that might be countered by different judgements from some other perspective; they are absolute claims. Things are as we say they are, or they are not.

But once we begin to reflect about truth in these ways, it can seem an impossibly ambitious notion. Our judgements that propositions are true are, after all, our judgements; they involve our thinking; they are not the verdict of some omniscient god who has direct access both to what we think and to how things are and can weigh them up. How could our thinking arrive at a standpoint beyond our thinking, from which to judge? And so we are immediately thrust into some of the deepest problems of the theory of knowledge.

If one assumes that these problems are insoluble, one is likely to conclude that whatever its pretensions to absolute status the notion of truth has to be relativized in some way or other. As we shall see in a moment, it would be better to give up any talk about truth at all, since relativized notions cannot deliver the goods we want the notion of truth to provide. But before we look at some alternatives, the point to grasp at the moment is simply that the notion of truth we do use does have this pretension to absoluteness. It does seek to compare how things are with how we think they are.

It is worth being a little more precise about the sort of comparison we require. Hirst (1974, ch. 5), for instance, has argued that traditional views of truth are impossible because they require a comparison of what we think with the world, presented neat, as it were, and unconceptualized. But that is not the sort of comparison we require; if it were we would indeed be in a hopeless state, since, as Hirst says, most, if not quite all, of our experience of the world is mediated by our conceptions of it. But we can still distinguish our thought, say, that pineapple juice curdles milk from our observation of what happens when we mix pineapple juice and milk. Our observation is indeed imbued with concepts, but it is quite distinct from the thought we are testing. Our thought can either be as observation reveals or other than observation reveals; we have two distinct items and can make the requisite comparison between them.

If we had allowed earlier that concepts themselves could be true or false, then Hirst's objection might have been somewhat stronger: observation is usually shot through with concepts so we would not be able to get outside our concepts to see whether they are true. But we did not allow that concepts could be true; it is what we do with concepts, the statements we make employing them, that are true or false, and so we do not have the sort of problem that Hirst supposed.

I have been rather short with this deep problem of how we can achieve simple absolute truth. We shall look at some aspects of it again later when we consider what our experience is like. For the time being, I have only wanted to show that some of the comparisons we need are available to us.

Sceptical Theories of Truth

As we have noted, many philosophers have doubted our ability to arrive at the simple but challenging notion of truth as set out above. Instead, they have suggested more modest notions that are within our powers and whose application matches, fairly well at least, what we want to do with truth. One such idea is that the most we can hope from truth is merely coherence with other beliefs; when we say that p is true all we are really claiming is that p is consistent with other claims we accept, or is not inconsistent with any such claims. Another idea that ordinary people often find attractive is that a true claim is one that can prove its worth in use; that truth is a matter of pragmatic utility. An even less specific account is offered by those who insist on speaking only of 'truth for' people; little is usually said about the 'true' portion, but the insistence is that we can only judge of truth for this person or group of people versus truth for that person or group: 'Lafite is better than Bull's Blood' is supposedly true for me, but not perhaps for the promoters of Hungarian wines.

Each of these competing views has a certain plausibility. Coherence with other accepted claims is a *sine qua non* for any proposition to be accepted, and inconsistency is a major reason for rejecting claims. A good number of claims are useful in practice, and this may seem a more important aspect of them than their strict truth or falsity. After all, we get by in many fields with theories that are known only to be approximations to the truth, that is to say, that are known to be strictly speaking false; and many people think religious belief is necessary for our sanity, or at least our morality, and use this to justify its place in schools, irrespective of its simple truth. Again, as my example may suggest, there are a good number of claims which it is plausible to regard as true for some but not for others. All the same, none of these views captures what it essential for truth, and so they should not be accepted as adequate explications of that notion.

I have already tried to ward off some of the sceptical doubts that can encourage these alternative accounts of truth. Here I want to show briefly how they fail to measure up to our ordinary demands on the notion of truth. Some of my arguments may appear to be attacking 'straw men' since I shall attribute to people views they are unlikely to espouse in cold blood. The point, however, is that if their views are seriously held they must in consistency accept these claims. Their failure to do so testifies to their good sense, but it is fatal for the views they maintain.

A proposition, p, can be consistent with a set of beliefs that A accepts but inconsistent with another set that B accepts; but p is either true or false, it cannot be both. Even if we know that q is true, the fact that p is consistent with q does not show that p is true too; all we can say is what we said above that if we know that q is true, then we know that p is false if it is inconsistent with q. But consistency is a quite different matter from truth.

So too is pragmatic utility. A false claim can be useful, and a true claim can be of no use at all. Two incompatible claims could both serve equally well in all our practical pursuits, but they couldn't both be true.

Finally, as we noted in the previous chapter, the general strategy of making truth relative undermines one of the main practical points of having the terms 'true' and 'false', viz. being able to distinguish mistakes. If 'true' can only be 'true for', we do not seem to have any way to distinguish cases where A thinks that p, and p, from those where A makes a mistake. Similarly we have no obvious way of acknowledging disagreements between people: when I say p and you say *not p* it looks to us that there is a disagreement, but on the relativistic notion of truth we seem forced to say that p is true for me but *not p* is true for you, and there is no disagreement left. One might prefer a world with no mistakes and disagreements, but this is rather too easy a way of achieving it. The relativist can of course acknowledge a difference: I accept p, you do not. His problem is to characterize this difference as a disagreement without any implicit appeal to notions of simple truth.

The extreme difficulty of avoiding the ordinary absolute notion of truth can be shown by a kind of turning of the tables upon proponents of the views we have mentioned. They say: truth is coherence, or utility, or relative to the speaker. Are we to take these claims themselves as true? Presumably we must, unless the theorists are lying or wasting our time. But then in what sense of 'true'? The ordinary simple absolute sense, or the sense they are each offering us of what truth really is? The obvious way of taking their remarks is the former, the ordinary simple absolute sense. But then the theorists have straightforwardly refuted themselves. They try to tell us that truth can only be coherence, utility, or what-have-you, but they want us to accept that claim itself as true in the ordinary sense they have rejected. If there are no simple truths, then 'truth is coherence' cannot be one either. If it is to be understood as a simple truth, there can be simple truths: so the various theories are in general wrong. (They may be salvaged as limited accounts of some bits of language or thought, but they had pretensions themselves, as general accounts of truth, and those pretensions have been shown to be vain.)

The unobvious way of taking what the theorists say is that these claims are true only in their sense of truth. I am inclined to say then: so what? I'm interested in the truth about truth, not some poor relation. But such a reaction looks rather too much like begging the question against the theorist. So let us persevere with the unobvious interpretations. Take coherence first: it is coherent with our accepted beliefs that truth is coherence with our accepted beliefs. But unfortunately it isn't. I have just presented some reasons for thinking that that view is not consistent with my accepted beliefs about some fundamental but elementary logical matters. (And in saying that, I am obviously falling back into the simple notion of truth; but that is precisely what I meant in saying it was inescapable.)

Let us try utility. It is useful to work with the thought that truth is a matter of practical utility. It is hardly obvious that it is. The cardinals who opposed Galileo were satisfied with stories about the heavens that did useful things like predicting eclipses and fixing the date of Easter; clearing away usable but utterly misguided theories such as Ptolemy's was a precondition for the advances made possible by Newton, with all the good, and ill, they have brought us. And once again, in disputing the acceptability of the pragmatist's social or historical claim, I am dealing in matters that can only be understood as simply true or false.

The problem with the relativistic notions of truth is to get a clear enough idea of what they involve. If statements are only true for individuals, then I deny that 'statements are only true for individuals' is true for me. If truth is said to be relative to something more subtle than individuals, then I think we should seek to uncover the confusions that lead to such claims, rather than pursue these types of reflexive argument. As we have seen, there are cases where it looks plausible to say that truth is relative, but this a misleading way of describing what is going on, because fundamentally there is no truth of the matter at all. When we acknowledge the complexity of many common propositions we may be able to restate in acceptable terms most of what people are getting at when they talk of relative truth.

Do We Need a Theory of Truth?

One of the basic ideas that underlies what I have been saying is that any problems there might be for talking about truth already infect the ordinary things we say. If 'It is true that p' creates a problem for you, so must the simple p itself. Talk about truth is a reflective, second-order activity, and easily encourages us to perceive problems; but the hubris we may discover inheres in our simple first-order statements themselves. The point can be made in terms of assertion: in asserting anything, we are asserting it as true. So if we cannot mean what we think we mean by saying 'It is true that p,' we cannot mean what we intend to mean simply by asserting p on its own.

In the course of this exposition of Mackie's 'comparison' theory of truth, we have briefly glanced at some other 'theories' of truth: coherence, pragmatist, and relativist theories. The point I have just been making is the grain of truth in another such theory, the redundancy theory, which goes on, falsely, to say that 'It is true that p' means the same as p. My earlier account denied that equivalence, but I have now endorsed the associated idea that talk of truth is always eliminable, which is to say that any problems with it are to be found in the propositions themselves. There are other theories of truth discussed in philosophy which have not got quite the popular appeal of those we have looked at. But perhaps the most famous theory has not been mentioned so far, namely the correspondence theory. Here the fundamental idea is that a proposition is true when it corresponds with the facts. That may seem to cover Mackie's account (though, as he says, being simply as things are is a pretty strong kind of correspondence) but its distinctiveness can be seen when we ask exactly what kind of correspondence is envisaged. Typically people have wanted to find a point by point mirroring of bits of the world by bits of the sentences used to express true or false propositions. Such a story might be plausible for maps, or perhaps for pictograms, but ordinary language works in very different ways from such things. And again, even with maps, it is extremely difficult to distinguish the kinds of correspondence required for truth from those that result in systematic error, without some tacit appeal to the simple comparison notion of truth I have offered. So while an unspecified correspondence may be innocuous, let us admit that what we want is to get things simply right, as the comparison account says, and let us note that we do not have to make false assumptions about one-to-one mappings between words (or components of propositions) and the world.

Truth, Logic and Education

Whether or not we go in for judging propositions true or false, truth matters vitally to us. In the previous chapter I illustrated educational concern for truth, and in this I have suggested in passing that inadequate conceptions of truth can distort or disable educational thinking. But more generally, learning, inquiry and criticism can all be regarded as activities centrally concerned to augment the number of true propositions or to sift out false ones from among our stock of beliefs. As such, these activities could do with a mechanism that transmits truth or falsehood.

Such mechanisms exist. They are the forms of valid deductive argument. As I briefly mentioned earlier, an argument is a sequence of statements consisting of premisses, conclusion, and the link of support between them. In a deductive argument the support is such that if the premisses were true then the conclusion would have to be true too. When you have such an argument, truth is transmitted from the set of premisses taken together to the conclusion; but, conversely, falsehood is transmitted from the conclusion back to the set of premisses taken together. If we have some truths, then using them as premisses in a deductive argument may yield a new truth; if a deductive argument yields a false conclusion we can be sure that at least one of its premisses is false too.

These two facts about deductively valid argument structures are continually being used in the enterprise of knowledge, both on the large-scale social side and in our individual attempts to refashion the web of our beliefs. Experimentation or theoretical criticism is very often a matter of deriving a prediction by valid argument from what has been proposed and looking to see whether that prediction holds; if it doesn't this is pretty damning for the theory in question. Similarly in our own personal grasp of the world around us we are constantly expecting things on the basis of what we already believe and correcting those beliefs when expectations are falsified, and these processes often mirror what explicit deductive argument would yield. As we shall see in more detail later, investigation in real life is complex and this picture of the trouble-free transmission of truth or falsehood is somewhat oversimplified, but simplifications have their uses. No map captures everything, but the existence of tides does not detract from the value of knowing what the coastline looks like.

Given both the fact that these mechanisms for the transmission of truth or falsehood exist, and that they are so pervasive in our cognitive lives, one might well think that the study of deductive logic should have a central role in any initiation into the cognitive enterprise. Schools, however, do not seem to see it that way. They often claim to teach people to reason better by teaching them particular subjects, but it seems that such teaching serves mainly to improve reasoning in the restricted areas in which it is taught. This is not so surprising, since no one ever draws students' attention to the general patterns that are the focus of deductive logic. It may also be true that some forms of non-deductive reasoning are peculiar to different subjects, but that is no reason for not doing what one could about those aspects that are general. As I have acknowledged regarding real life investigation, real life arguments are not so easy to handle as the disinfected simplifications of formal logic, so the subject of deductive logic as an aid to reasoning would not be so cut-and-dried as it might appear; but again this is hardly a reason for not tackling it. Whether or not you are finally convinced that the notion of simple truth is one that it would be worth introducing to students in school in the hope of forestalling the confusion we can see around us, I do think we have here the beginnings of a case for much more serious consideration of the proper place of reasoning in the curriculum (cf. Brandon, 1985b).

Besides transmitting truth, we might like a mechanism for discovering truths in the first place. The possibility, or rather the general impossibility, of such a mechanism is one of the main themes of the theory of knowledge and since it is not really part of my brief to argue for a place for logic in schools, let us move on to consider knowledge.

3

Knowledge

Considerate la vestra semenza:
Fatti non fosse a viver come bruti
Ma per seguir virtute e conoscenza[3]

The preceding reflections on truth should suggest that while a concern for truth is a concern that may well stir up much of what is taken for granted by most people, it is one that will focus our attention on the various different sorts of proposition that we claim to know. Truth is a simple and sharp-edged weapon, but it is not itself a notion that we need to dwell on. Rather we have to turn to the different things that we claim to know.

Epistemological Questions

While some of the questions we looked at in the first chapter were phrased in terms of truth, what is common to virtually all of them is the question of the nature of our knowledge: what is it like and where is it to be found? The teachers Haes questioned differed on these issues: some thought that knowledge is fixed and certain, others said it was provisional; some thought that science and mathematics are our paradigm cases of genuine knowledge, but many other people would wish to include moral or religious claims as equally reliable. We can see large parts of the philosophical tradition as answers to such questions. Many philosophers have told us what knowledge is like – how it is based, or what its logical relations are to other concepts such as belief. Again a great deal of philosophy

28

focuses on the reliability of knowledge – in some cases, philosophers have questioned virtually everything we believe: 'stage' philosophers are still often shown wondering whether they are indeed standing on a stage. But most philosophers have in fact accepted many of the beliefs they found around them. Their scepticism has been partial, a matter of querying or rejecting some of the beliefs in common currency, not all. Lucretius praised Epicurus for freeing mankind from the terrors of superstition; Locke sought to free science from 'pretenders to a knowledge they had not' ([1690] 1961, III, viii, 2); and modern philosophy is full of the same concern for cognitive health.

As I said earlier, I cannot here go into particular cases such as psychoanalysis or Marxism or theism. Nor do I think there is much for you to gain from an extended discussion of the logical links between our concept of knowledge and our other concepts. But we can usefully survey the fundamental logical structure of our knowledge itself. This will yield insight into its status and so help in deciding what would be the most appropriate attitudes for teachers to adopt towards the transmission of our knowledge. While we shall not be able to discuss any of the more detailed questions fully you will see that the general survey of the structure of knowledge does provide a suggestive framework in which to take those discussions further.

The Word 'Know'

Before beginning with that task, however, I must indicate some of the restrictions on the scope of the discussion. I am concerned with the sort of knowledge that involves truth; the sort that when you know something, you know the truth, or at least a bit of the truth. In English we use the word 'know' and its cognates much more widely. One crude classification of our usage distinguishes between

(1) knowledge by acquaintance: know NP;
(2) practical knowledge: know how to VP;
(3) propositional knowledge: know that p.

As is commonly the case, virtually the same information can often be conveyed in what are logically or linguistically very different ways. We could report that Tom knows Pythagoras' theorem, or that Tom knows how to calculate the area of the square on the hypotenuse of a right-angled triangle, given the squares on the other two sides, or that Tom knows that the square on the hypotenuse of a right-angled triangle is equal to the sum of the squares on the other two sides. In other cases, such as 'Fred knows London like the back of his hand', it is not so easy to find these alternative paraphrases. But my main concern at the moment is for you to realize that I am only going to talk about the third of the kinds of knowledge, propositional knowledge.

Empirical and *A Priori* Knowledge

Restricting ourselves to propositional knowledge there is an important *prima facie* distinction to be made between items of knowledge that can be established simply on the basis of reflection or calculation and items of knowledge that require some sort of experience or observation. Pythagoras' theorem, or more strictly the fact that Pythagoras' theorem is deducible from certain sets of geometrical axioms, is something that can be established simply by reasoning. The area of the cricket pitch at Sabina Park is something you would have to go and look at to find out. The fact that all bachelors are unmarried is again something that can be established (assuming certain restrictions on the sense of the word 'bachelor') simply by reflecting on the standard meaning of the words used, whereas the claim that all such bachelors are generally more contented with life than their married counterparts is something whose truth or falsity requires extensive and complex investigation of the world, after one has clarified the senses of the words it contains.

Traditionally philosophers have used the terms '*a priori*' to label the first sort of knowledge, the sort that can be established by reason alone, and '*a posteriori*' or 'empirical' to label the other sort. (Notice that this is a much wider use of the word 'empirical' than the one with which you may be familiar, and that it has no evaluative connotations.) I said above that the distinction is a *prima facie* one because there is a great deal of involved argument in modern philosophy about whether there really is such a distinction, although everyone can agree about where many items of knowledge would go if there were. In terms of school subjects, *a priori* knowledge is represented pre-eminently by mathematics (to which we may add logic), while everything else that is clearly propositional knowledge would count as *a posteriori* – chemistry, history, etc. As far as we are concerned, it is not necessary to enter into the debates about the distinction; again my only concern is that you recognize that I am talking about *a posteriori* or empirical knowledge. I have nothing to say about mathematics or logic. (I suspect a lot of what I do say could be applied without much revision to those subjects, but the issues are very complex and controversial, and anyway I do not think they raise problems for teachers in the way that empirical knowledge does.)

Empirical Knowledge and Experience

So our concern from now on will be with empirical knowledge. That is a big enough field. It includes items like 'Hydrogen has three isotopes', 'Mozart wrote forty-one symphonies', 'I have a feeling that I'm going to sneeze', 'Rewards promote learning more than threats', and so on and so on.

As was obvious from the account I gave above, empirical knowledge has got something to do with our experience or observation. Our reasons for accepting particular items of empirical knowledge will often be a matter of sensory experience, although in practice we both take a lot on trust and would anyway be unable to have direct sensory inputs – neither the past nor the hidden structures of physical or some sociological theories are directly observable. But let us pause a moment to consider those cases where we do have fairly direct sensory input.

Perhaps the main point to be made is that we can distinguish between thinking that p and having an experience that p. For us, having an experience usually combines these two aspects: sensory experiences and judgements about the kind of experience it is. This point cropped up earlier when we glanced at one of Hirst's arguments about truth. You can think that the cat is on the mat and you can see that the cat is on the mat (and you might be able to hear or feel by touch that the cat is on the mat). And these are distinguishable things, even when they are bound together in reflective self-conscious experience. All of them involve the employment of concepts, as we say. Thinking about cats on mats involves the use of concepts of cats, mats and spatial relations, and experiencing cats on mats similarly employs one's conceptual resources. Experience only rarely comes unconceptualized, and when it does what have been called 'raw feels' do not tell you anything; we have to start thinking to get anywhere with them.

I hope those last remarks sounded plausible. We easily talk about concepts, but it is by no means clear what that talk really amounts to. In the case of thinking, and in the human case, we can get a long way by replacing talk of concepts with attention to how people use language; but the two things are not the same. And in the case of perception or sensory experience it is by no means clear how what we call concepts relate to language or how they develop. While much epistemological work has tried to solve this problem of the origin of concepts, we can afford to leave it aside. The point to remember is that we don't really meet with unconceptualized experience, so concepts of some sort are a given of our story. But as I said earlier, the main point I want to stress is that there is a difference between an experience and the thought (knowledge) that is associated with it. There is then a gap between seeing and believing, in logic if not in our too credulous practice.

Public Knowledge

There is, however, one aspect of the question about the origin and development of our concepts that is worth a brief mention. Even though each of us has to acquire our concepts somehow, they are not our private creations. This is patently obvious when we translate talk of concepts into talk about the languages we use. Children have to learn their mother tongue, but they don't invent it; it is there already, publicly available and publicly learnable. Languages, and by extension our concepts, are social facts, not purely personal. While it is important in general philosophy to ponder precisely what this implies, and what it doesn't imply, I am concerned now to make an analogous point about our knowledge. Most of our stock of knowledge is not derived from our own unaided investigations. We take it on trust; we take it over from other people, books, and other sources. While schools still insist on individuals cramming their heads full of diverse scraps of information, in the rest of real life what often matters much more is what is known rather than what John or Mary knows. Popper (1972) has appropriated the popular but unclear contrast between subjective and objective matters to label this impersonal knowledge stored in libraries and data banks 'objective knowledge'. Perhaps it is safer to call it 'impersonal knowledge'; but the point remains that whatever you call it such knowledge is what matters most, both to institutionalized science and to bureaucracies. This fact reflects one important aspect of the social basis of our knowledge; another that we shall meet later is the tradition of criticism or testing. In both respects, the progressive development of knowledge is not usually a solitary pursuit, but a social one. It flourishes in certain kinds of social environment and not in others; indeed it has flourished in a very unusual context, though one that has now become so entrenched for most of us that we may have difficulty in realizing its peculiarity.

These facts underlie one aspect of this discussion that may be worrying you. We have plunged right in to the middle of the cognitive enterprise. We have not tried to find some specially reliable starting point or foundation. In philosophy the idea that we must have such foundations has been very influential; but it does not correspond to most people's engagement with knowledge. Rather we start from where our peers are. Most people, most social groups, stay there, but we are focusing on the procedures of groups who are committed to criticizing and revising their starting points.

The facts that the crucial kinds of knowledge are impersonal and that changes are socially produced do not make some kinds of concern for 'personal' knowledge irrelevant. While it is more sensible to go to the metereological office to find out whether the sun was shining on 16 July 1982 in Kingston than to rely on one's memory, that is not the end of it. Knowledge gets into the impersonal stores from people, or instruments. And the knowledge in the data banks is only as reliable as the 'personal' knowledge of those people or machines when they fed it in. If one learnt that the person making the records was incompetent, or that the machine taking readings was malfunctioning, then out goes that impersonal knowledge.

So the importance of impersonal knowledge or, more generally, the pervasiveness of our reliance on testimony, does not mean that we should ignore some traditional concerns for reliability. We have procedures for checking whether machines are working properly, we have rough guides for deciding when to accept and when to doubt what other people tell us. Later on I shall say a little about how I would prefer to see these caveats about the move from evidence or testimony to our conclusions; for the time being the point is that they do not cease to be important because it does not matter which of us, if any, carries the knowledge in our heads. What does drop out is the philosophical doctrine that genuine knowledge carries some special 'inner' mark or feeling of certainty.

Knowledge and Authority

I have just said that we have guidelines to tell us when to accept and when not to accept what other people report. Different groups have different guides. To put it another way, different groups recognize different sorts of authority in their dealings with knowledge. Many people require claims to be consistent with the 'testimony' of their own senses. Many people allow claims made in certain special places to override all other considerations – so what it says in the Bible, or in Aristotle, is accepted, whatever other reasons there are against it. On the account I shall be giving of the structure of knowledge, none of these moves is acceptable. But of course I am making a normative claim, I am saying that you ought not to give authority to these kinds of factor; I am not describing what you do, since I have just acknowledged that many people do things that I regard as irrelevant if knowledge is their goal. But that doesn't mean we have an arbitrary choice here. Rather the account I give is meant to be an accurate description of the logical structure of at least a central part of the knowledge all of us have; the normative claims arise from my belief that this description applies to all the knowledge we could have and that therefore the kinds of authority I am rejecting have no reasoned basis in the nature of knowledge, however useful they might fortuitously have been.

Singular and General

With these preliminaries briefly mentioned, let us move on to giving this description of the logical structure of our knowledge. First we need to grasp a logical distinction. It is, if you like, a numerical distinction: between one and more than one. A proposition can tell us about one individual – a place, person, or thing – or it can tell us about more than one individual. Part of a proposition can pick out one individual – a definite description such as 'the present Prime Minister of Jamaica', or a proper name in context such as 'Edward Seaga' – or it can introduce more than one into our thinking, like plural noun phrases such as 'capitalist running-dogs'. We can label these contrasts, 'singular', on the one hand, 'general' on the other. When we are dealing with whole propositions we can go on to distinguish several sorts of general statement, or generalization. So we can have a series starting with a logically singular proposition such as 'Today is sunny', and then move through various generalizations from the weakest, 'existential' generalization, 'At least one day is sunny' (this is the precise content that modern logic gives to English sentences such as 'Some days are sunny'), through various proportional generalizations such as 'A few days are sunny', 'Many days are sunny', 'Most days are sunny', or their more sophisticated statistical counterparts like '84 per cent of days are sunny', to the strongest, 'universal' generalization, 'All days are sunny'. Here you can see that the singular statement picks on one particular day; the other statements do not in that way focus on one particular day, since even the existential generalization doesn't tell you which day or days it is talking about. I have indicated the different kinds of generalization we can form and the names I would call them, but for this discussion the two most important kinds are the existential and the universal generalizations.

One small point which is worth getting out of the way is the fact that we can generalize in two contexts, which can be called 'open' and 'closed'. The sentences I have used above about sunny days might well be used in a conversational context in which it was clear that only the last five years at one particular place were in question. They would then be talking about a limited set of just over 1,800 days, and one could go through every day to check on their truth. This sort of context yields closed generalizations; what is called the 'universe of discourse' is finite and enumerable. But in many other cases we generalize about an unlimited set which we could not go through one by one. If we say that aspirins relieve headaches we are talking about a potentially endless stream of aspirins and we are prepared to say of other things that if they were aspirins they would relieve headaches too. In such cases we are using open generalizations; and these cases are the norm.

Concepts, Generality and Revision

Having got the distinction clear, we can now see the first important point that our concepts are, at least in most cases, general. We have a concept of fraternity or of sugar or of a whale. These do not introduce individuals into our thinking but rather kinds of relation between people, or a kind of stuff, or a kind of animal. There can be many such animals or many lumps of the stuff, and the use of the concept is not tied to any one particular animal or lump. We can say that the use of such concepts is tantamount to accepting some implicit generalizations about different individual animals or lumps of stuff all having certain properties in common. (This might be an oversimplification, but we are always having to simplify to make progress.)

A very important aspect of the pursuit of knowledge is the attempt to make explicit these sorts of generalization embedded in the use of concepts. This attempt almost always leads us to change our use in some respects. It is well known that whales were once classified as fish, but are now grouped under mammals. You might want to say that we changed our concept of fish or of whales or perhaps of both; the point is that such a change, however described, was encouraged by our attempts to arrive at perspicuous generalizations about the animals in question. In fact, revision of the network of concepts and making statements using those concepts go hand in hand; it is usually fruitless simply to set out a taxonomy without at the same time using it to make new and better generalizations. As Whewell said, 'the establishment of a right definition of a term may be a useful step in the explication of our conceptions; but this will be the case only when we have under consideration some proposition in which the term is employed' (quoted in Mill [1843], 1886, IV, ch. 4; see also Flew, 1975, ch. 5, for some trenchant and sensible remarks about definitions). And so one may wonder, for instance, whether anything is gained by arguing about the class structure of a society if nothing more is to be said about that society and its workings. Similar doubts arise about the ritual 'definitions of terms' students are often encouraged to put at the beginning of their essays.

I have said that it is typical of the advance of knowledge in any area to revise the conceptual scheme that common sense provides. Of course, common sense doesn't stand still, and for some people in some areas it is more sophisticated, more up to date, than for other people or in other areas. But the general point is obvious enough, and no one could deny its applicability at least to the natural sciences and mathematics. In other areas it may not seem so clearly relevant, but I suspect that this is due to the greater complexities of such areas and our general lack of success in developing theoretical understanding of them. But whether or not general agreement is achieved, it is clear that people do seek to revise and stipulate technical meanings for terms like 'revolution' or 'learning' or 'social class'. All this transmuting of ordinary language into technical terms does, however, create a general problem for teachers. People do not normally like to revise their conceptual inheritance. What is implicit takes a lot of painful extracting, and so it tends to remain undisturbed as long as possible. It is also, of course, what is learnt first. I suspect that by no means enough is done to make students face the fact that they are being required to change their concepts, to learn a bit of new language, if you like (cf. Holton, 1984, esp. p. 103). Teachers are often encouraged to make new learning appear 'relevant' to the learner and this is also likely to underplay the discontinuities between the learner's common sense and the actual content to be learnt.

In any case there is plenty of evidence that students do not learn what they are expected to learn in such cases of conceptual revision. It has been found, for instance, that high-school students of physics think about everyday problems in the pre-Newtonian implicit physics of our ignorant common sense rather than in the somewhat more accurate terms of their school specialization (McCloskey, 1983). And, to mention a case I have observed, some students in maths are determined to believe that division by zero is a possible operation, even if it doesn't yield any answer, rather than grasp the stipulation of the subject that such an operation is simply undefined. In these and many other cases, it seems that students persist in thinking in terms that common sense allows rather than face the fact that they have to uproot and destroy these bits of their inheritance.

Aiming at Understanding

I have said that typically conceptual or taxonomic revision proceeds hand in hand with the reformulation, correction or discovery of generalizations. Typically, again, we seek such generalizations in order to understand more of what is going on. This is true, I think, even in areas that may seem preoccupied with taxonomy such as some parts of biology, but it is perhaps more obvious in subjects like chemistry. You find two lumps of stuff that look and smell alike and that you initially classify as the same substance, but then you discover that one lump behaves one way in a certain solution while the other does something different. You are likely to reclassify your lumps into at least two substances so that you can get a firmer grip on understanding these and other reactions. And when you have a generalization, you want to understand it too in its turn. So you are likely to put forward further generalizations to do so, since understanding, as I briefly mentioned earlier, is in large part a matter of seeing how things connect and can be unified. The fact that disparate items can be unified in this way is in turn one of the main reasons for thinking that the explanation is on the right lines.

If you want to understand why acids turn litmus paper red you have to do something to link acids and litmus paper and colour changes and all these to other things you know. The strategy that we have found to be of enormous value in doing this is to postulate initially hidden levels of structure – so now we would talk of molecules, or ions, or shells of electrons surrounding the nucleus, and these notions serve to link the odd case of litmus paper to a vast range of other phenomena. We can see the same sorts of connections in a quite different case: we want to understand why poorer families tend to have more children, and we may seek to show how children are a more sensible investment for poor people than for more affluent groups. Whether or not this is the correct account in any particular case, it exemplifies the way we try to put the phenomenon to be explained into a wider picture: in this case, of means–end rationality. Here we may not be going to a different level of structure as we did in moving from everyday substances to their molecular structure, but we are at least moving to a more general factor, something that can be seen at work in other instances besides family size.

Explaining Away

One central purpose then in our cognitive endeavours is to get hold of explanations and the understanding they bring. But as I have said, many of our successes here have involved moving away from the way things appear to us to be towards underlying structures or mechanisms that certainly do not appear on the surface. Accompanying these moves we also very often find that the appearances are 'explained away'; the deeper explanatory picture we arrive at allows us to do without notions that might have been suggested by the surface appearances. Just as we can successfully explain away the strong impression we all have that the earth is standing still and go on to endorse a theory which says that it is moving in a very complicated and, by our ordinary standards, remarkably rapid manner, so we can equally well see how to dispense with many of the appearances around us, from intrinsic colours-as-seen to the equal opportunities many people imagine they have. Our best explanations do not need to postulate these items; the story they tell is, then, in conflict with our unreflective common sense.

This suggestion relies, of course, on the idea that you should get rid of what you do not need. Such an injunction is not logically forced upon us, but it would seem to be the only reasonable course to adopt. Once one has given up any belief that merely being inherited as part of one's conceptual resources bestows any authority upon a concept or a proposition then it seems nothing remains to justify using such resources but their contribution to one's cognitive tasks.

Once again we have a problem that schools seem not to face. While they are prepared to bemoan supposed moral decadence in the surrounding society, in most other respects schools like to think they are in harmony with their clients, or at least their clients' parents. But if they were to set out to inculcate the best understanding we have of the world, they would continually be running up against and denying beliefs which these parents hold, at least implicitly.

For the same kind of reasons as I mentioned in connection with conceptual revisions, school subjects often seem to underplay their differences from what their students think. Or they are distorted in related ways. Thus a lot of science teaching is bifurcated, with one aspect focusing on limited things that can be done in a school laboratory and observed without much sophistication, and another, apparently quite unrelated aspect, in which the teacher reports on what the theorists are saying (or, rather, were saying some years before). Eddington's or Russell's success as popularizers of science owed a lot, I think, to their insistence on the challenge science offers to our ordinary views: you think you are sitting at a solid table, but really it is mostly empty space. I suspect our teaching of science in the schools could benefit from a return to such challenges, rather than pretending that they do not exist.

And of course it is not only science where the pursuit of knowledge undermines popular prejudice. History does not leave much of nationalistic or patriotic belief standing secure, and the social sciences rarely agree with the claims of politicians or the spokespeople of the status quo. (I am here talking simply about the facts of the matter, for example what a country's war aims were, or whether certain people are being discriminated against; not about disagreements on which policies to pursue.) And perhaps one of the most controversial cases is the problem of religion. But for the moment, the point has been made that explanatory knowledge challenges popular belief rather more than schools seem willing to acknowledge.

The Asymmetry of Verification and Falsification

We have been looking at the ramifications of the fact that our concepts can be seen to involve implicit generalizations. We can now move on to the second major logical point about our knowledge. There is a simple logical fact at the root of our reflections about human knowledge of the world: logically singular claims can falsify but not verify open universal generalizations. To take a popular and simple example, 'That swan is not white' (which is logically a singular statement) falsifies, is logically incompatible with, the open universal generalization, 'All swans are white'; but however many different claims like 'This swan is white', 'That swan is white', 'The next swan is white', etc., you collect, they do not serve to verify, they do not logically force upon you the universal generalization, 'All swans are white.' And a good thing too, since we know a few swans that are not white.

To put it in terms of logical entailments, 'This X is not Y' entails 'It is not the case that all Xs are Y' whereas any number of claims like 'This X is Y' do not entail 'All Xs are Y'. The singular claim entails the negation of a universal generalization, but no collection of singular claims ever entails a universal generalization itself. It is worth noting that the negation of a universal generalization only amounts to an existential generalization: 'It is not the case that all Xs are Y' is equivalent to 'At least one X is not Y'.

So much is a simple matter of logic. How does this relate to the human predicament? We have already noted that empirical knowledge connects in some way with observation and experience. We cannot discover or intuit how things are simply by thinking about them; we are forced to investigate; we are forced to rely at some point on the evidence of our senses or of our machines. And when we do so, what they reveal is something that is logically singular. We see that today is sunny or we smell that room 12 has got hydrogen sulphide in it or we hear that the baby is crying or the seismograph records a particularly strong tremor. The judgements we make on the basis of this sort of evidence are about what is happening at a particular place and time, or at least they would be if we were scrupulous about them. You might boil mercury and report what the boiling point of mercury is; your report would be logically a universal generalization to the effect that mercury always boils at such and such a temperature (in certain standard conditions of pressure, etc.); but strictly speaking what you are really in a position to report is that one sample of mercury boiled at such and such a temperature, and that is logically singular. And in other contexts, you would be less inclined to jump from your observations to general claims – if you see people demonstrating in the street, you are not likely to claim that all people, or even all people looking like those you can see, spend their time demonstrating. So what observation or experience reveals is singular.

But as we saw above, what we want is explanatory understanding, and that requires strong generalizations. People argue whether proportional or statistical generalizations can really explain things, but I think everyone is agreed that some sorts of what I have called 'universal' generalization can do that job. If it is true that unlike magnetic poles attract each other, then, given various standing conditions, you have an explanation why a magnetic compass keeps pointing north, and why this one does, and that one, and the next one. We shall return to generalizations that are weaker than universal ones; for the time being let us simplify and sharpen our problem by restricting ourselves to universal generalizations.

We can now see the relevance of the logical fact to our

knowledge. We want universal generalizations, but what we have to use can only produce singular claims. The logical fact tells us that no matter how many singular claims we can collect, they will never logically entail one of the universal generalizations we want. We cannot get a logical guarantee that our generalizations are as safe as our evidence. We cannot have a device for generating the true premisses we referred to at the end of the previous chapter.

Methodological Responses

There are two things we can do in this predicament. We could try to find ways of making our generalizations as safe as possible, given our evidence. We might hope to discover some sort of 'inductive logic' that could guide us in moving from singular claims to the sorts of generalization we want. People differ on the cost effectiveness of this reaction. We know that any such inductive logic will be unable to guarantee success; we know also from the attempts made along these lines that it will be a pretty complicated affair; and we know, from a consideration I shall come to later, that there are very important areas where it can hardly hope to guide us. But despite these difficulties, most people think there is something to be done here – some moves from evidence to conclusion seem a lot more sensible than others, and we ought to be able to say why and to organize such reasons into a fairly neat system.

But there is another reaction to the situation. So far we have been stressing what we logically cannot do – we cannot derive universal generalizations validly from our singular claims. But the logical fact has another side to it: we can validly deduce the negation of universal generalizations; we can throw out generalizations, even if we cannot rule them in. So instead of concentrating on arriving at generalizations, we could focus our attention on rejecting inadequate generalizations. We can then be as reckless as we like about coming up with generalizations, so long as we are careful to test them rigorously, that is to say, to test them in such a way that they are likely to be falsified if they are false.

If we follow this path, we will not need to seek any sort of guarantee for our generalizations; we will instead seek to be as harsh as we can with them so that we can weed out inadequate ones. In the terms that Popper has made famous (1959, or, more generally accessible, 1969), we can see the history of knowledge as a matter of conjecture and refutation. Or, in more familiar terms, we can see in this reaction an endorsement of the centrality of a kind of trial and error to our knowledge of the world.

It is worth noting that these two reactions are not mutually exclusive. We can think it worthwhile to take care about the formulation of new generalizations and we can hope for an inductive logic to help us in this task, while still acknowledging the comparative strength of refutations. But there is another consideration that makes the second, Popperian, reaction seem much more pertinent.

Depth of Understanding

I have already mentioned the fact that one of the most powerful means of achieving explanatory understanding has been to postulate new structures. This profoundly changes the logical situation we looked at above. In the simple case of the swans, the terms occurring in the singular claims and in the universal generalizations were the same ('swan' and 'white'); it is intuitively obvious how the universal claim is a generalization of the various singular claims we mentioned. But when, for instance, we explain the distribution of eye colour in different generations by reference to different genes, we now have quite different terms in the singular claims from those in the generalizations ('blue eyes', 'brown eyes' in the singular claims; 'gene 1', 'gene 2' and talk of dominant and recessive genes, etc. in the generalizations).

Putting it crudely, the two sides of the fence are now 'This X is Y' and 'All Z are W'; and there are no direct logical linkages left: neither verification nor falsification. There is simply no way to move logically from talk of X and Y to talk of Z and W, or vice versa. But of course, that is putting it too crudely. The explanations we offer do bridge this gap, and they do it in various and often complex ways; but in the simplified terms of our logical schema, what these links amount to are claims such as 'All Z are X', and 'All W and Y'. But while we can reinstate logical links between our singular claims and our explanatory generalizations, the main thing to realize is that talk about our Zs and Ws is not directly suggested to us by what we start from, the talk of Xs and Ys. Someone has to invent the idea, of molecules or genes or rules of transformational grammar, or whatever, and of how these 'new' things behave. None of this is given directly by the phenomenon to be explained, and it is very difficult to see how general formal rules, such as an inductive logic might aspire to offer, could ever begin to help in finding such ideas. But, as I've said, it is these ideas that have proven explanatorily powerful; and they can apparently only come as creative conjectures. So perhaps we should put most of our eggs in that basket.

One lesson of all this is that cognitive revision involves both creative conjectures – 'divergent' thinking in Hudson's (1967) terms – and critical testing, which requires careful 'convergent' thinking. To the extent that schools cultivate only one kind of thinking, people are not being helped to participate fully in our cognitive life. Again, while both sorts are necessary it would be salutary not to confuse them as so often happens. Students are asked to 'deduce' things in a comprehension exercise or in a laboratory experiment that can only be hypothesized, while there are other things that can in fact be deductively inferred. Not to see that different skills are involved can only hinder fruitful teaching here.

The issue we have just been looking at is often portrayed as the existence of a distinction between observational and theoretical terms. I have tried to explain it without making that connection explicit, though it may well have occurred to you: we observe blue eyes, we don't observe genes. But of course, there's a problem with this way of putting the issue: some people these days do observe genes, just as other people observe muons and other sub-atomic particles. I have mentioned already that in some cases you will be likely to claim that you have seen or measured the boiling point of mercury in general, when what you have actually seen or measured is only a singular occurrence of this sample of mercury boiling at this place and time. But since we think this measurement is reliable, your report incorporates a lot of these assumptions of reliability; you stick your neck out, without even noticing it on many occasions. And similarly with so-called theoretical terms: if someone grasps the theory and thinks it sufficiently reliable, he will report his observations in terms of that theory, rather than redescribe them in less ambitious ways. We can always move down towards more generally accepted claims if we have to; but in general we try to stay with the most powerful and informative ways of expressing them, and these will be the ones incorporating what we currently deem to be reliable theory.

The Role of Background Assumptions

I have said that the most important point here is that the ideas incorporated in the generalizations are conjectures going beyond anything in the singular data. Another crucial fact is that the logical links are now between singular data and a set of generalizations, many of which are usually left pretty unspecific. When we only had 'This swan is not white' and 'All swans are white', the former directly refutes the latter so if you accept the former you cannot accept the latter. But when schematically the situation is 'This X is not Y' on the one hand and 'All Z are W, and all X are Z, and all W are Y' on the other then the first claim only shows that there is error somewhere in the set of generalizations, in the theory; it doesn't tell us where. The only way we can now chalk up a refutation of the theoretical claim, 'All Z are W', is to assume that the other generalizations, the ones that link theory to observation, are all correct. And that is obviously a pretty large assumption.

We can in fact go back to the simple example and find similar difficulties. We took as a given of that elementary situation the singular claim, 'This swan is not white'. But, to be strict with ourselves, our evidence may be less ambitiously stated as 'Jim observed that this swan is not white'. The claim about the swan is itself based on visual evidence available to Jim. But to get from the visual evidence to the claim about the swan in the objective world, or vice versa, we similarly would need various linking claims. We assume things about the way light behaves, we assume things about Jim's normality as an observer. We certainly cannot infer validly from the report of what Jim saw that what he reported to have seen was in fact the case. (This claim may need some qualifications in the light of how we sometimes use our language here, but my point could have been made equally well by retreating yet further down the line to the very weak, but perhaps most honest, claim that it appeared to Jim that he saw a swan that was not white: nothing follows from this about what colour the swan was; there might not even have been a swan at all.) So we can now see that even in the apparently simplest cases, we make a lot of assumptions in using singular claims to weed out our generalizations. Of course, we still cannot verify any of our universal generalizations, but we can now see how provisional even our refutations have become. They are at the mercy of these varied assumptions that bridge the various gaps we have uncovered.

It should be noted that in talking of assumptions or background knowledge here I am not suggesting that these items have any particularly privileged position. They are not immune from critical examination. Our position is that any claim to knowledge can be examined, but that it is not possible to test all of them at once. To examine a claim you must take other claims for granted, for the time being. Of course many of the assumptions referred to in the preceding discussion are so deep-rooted and inarticulate that it may be misleading to call them 'theory', but this does not affect the logic of the situation.

A different way of describing the situation, in terms of observational terms, is that our use of observational terms is logically no more secure than that of theoretical terms. The provisional, conjectural status we have seen in theoretical generalizations inheres equally in the singular observations we make, though in practice we rarely notice this, since we take a great deal of our knowledge as finally settled. Few people realize that they are making a theoretical leap in talking about the sun yesterday and today. But it is a theoretical, non-observational claim that there is one persistent object that 'rises' each day (or at least it was until very recently), and it is a theoretical claim that has occasionally been rejected, as in Xenophanes' cosmology. A much more pertinent area in which to see the provisional status of singular observations is that of scientific measuring techniques. One important achievement in the natural sciences (and one of their differences from much of our study of ourselves) is to have gained an understanding of how their measuring instruments work. But of course that understanding is a matter of conjectural theory, and there are occasions when we have had to revise singular measurements because we have come to revise the theories built into the measurement techniques. Thus when it was realized that the concentration of radio-carbon in the atmosphere has not been constant we had to revise a large number of radio-carbon dates, and with them our provisional theories of European prehistory (Renfrew, 1976).

We have only taken the first steps in complicating the account of cognitive revision. It might be more realistic to see change in terms of Lakatos' (1970) 'research programmes' rather than isolated claims; and one should acknowledge that there are several ways in which history has been a lot messier and a lot more lucky than my picture suggests. In making these admissions it is important, I

46

believe, to tread a path between the tendency to think in terms of a framework within which people operate (which is a reasonable description of what we do) and the logical point that propositions belonging to such frameworks are no different from those within them, so that frameworks are not immune to criticism.

The Falsification of Less than Universal Generalizations

In the preceding section we have seen that the neat asymmetry between verification and falsification with which we started has been radically modified, since falsification is now only relative to assumed background knowledge. While I have been avoiding the complexities of open proportional or statistical generalizations, it is worth noting here that they also involve a similar relativizing of falsification. (Verification remains as impossible as ever.) In this case, falsification is only possible given some decisions about sampling and about how unlikely one wants errors to be. The reason can easily be seen. While one black swan refutes the universal generalization, 'All swans are white', how many do we need to refute the weaker 'Most swans are white'? You have to make some choices about the kind of sample you will allow to exclude the generalization in question. Given some such decisions, observing 73 per cent non-white swans in a large random sample would be taken to rule out the generalization; but it cannot do so absolutely. Even if most swans are white, it is still possible to get a random sample that is mostly non-white; it is just rather unlikely.

Description or Recommendation?

I have presented a picture of our knowledge that may well seem unfamiliar to you. Even if you are prepared to accept it for some specialized and perhaps peripheral areas, you are not likely to think that it is a correct description of most of what we all claim to know. What reply can I make to such criticism?

In the first place, we have to distinguish here, as elsewhere, between what we think we know about our knowledge and what, if anything, we really do know about it. Knowledge is as hidden by

47

ideology as the rest of our social being; you should not be surprised if knowledge turns out to be somewhat different from what you unreflectively imagine.

In the second place, I would claim to have delineated the fundamental logical structures inherent in the propositions we believe or claim to know. If I am right, it doesn't matter that we do not recognize these logical structures; they are there, and put their limits on what we can, as a matter of logic, achieve. Our untutored thinking bears often only a tenuous relation to what the science of logic reveals. So in saying that I am talking about the logical structuring of our knowledge, I am not committed to any claims about how in practice we think or go about revising our beliefs. Given the largely negative achievements logic allows us, I would not even claim that what I have said tells us how we ought to proceed, except perhaps in criticizing others. We might well come upon the truth by ignoring everything I have said. Since no method can guarantee success, to that extent Feyerabend's 'Anything goes!' strategy (Feyerabend, 1975) might do as well as any other; though few would think we should be so carefree in the pursuit of knowledge.

But in the third place, I would want to say that a lot of our actual thinking does in fact reflect the logical principles I have been discussing. You think that if it has rained recently the lawn will be wet and when you find the lawn bone dry you conclude that despite the dark clouds it didn't rain. You may not have arrived at this conclusion by any process that involves what logicians call *modus tollens* – the principle that *if p then q* and *not q* together entail *not p* – but it is certainly as if you had. You are playing around with a new machine and find that pressing a particular button always seems to produce a recognizable result, a beep for instance, so you begin to call it a beep button; that description incorporates the hypothesis you have to some extent tested in your interactions with the machine. These are deliberately trivial examples, but they are meant only to show that some of the processes I have been discussing are in fact pervasive features of our everyday thinking.

Although our ordinary thinking does in fact mirror a lot of the epistemology I have been expounding, it may often, as I have admitted, not in any sense be based upon it. And of course your objection started from the fact that much of our thinking does not seem to fit the picture. This is one reason why the revision of knowledge is in fact so social a matter. Each one of us may have the most diverse and logically unsupportable views about what we believe but the social institution of inquiry produces outcomes somewhat more in accordance with the picture I have sketched. So whatever individuals may think about their particular views, the institution by and large takes the tentativeness of claims for granted. It keeps rewriting its history, as Kuhn (1970) stressed, to make the present contenders look virtually inevitable; but in another generation the picture will be redrawn. (I must acknowledge that this discourse too is part of such a history – what epistemology can do for teachers will no doubt look very different to other philosophers or at other times.) Rivalry between scholars or scientists may often degenerate into mud-slinging or other unfortunate forms, but it can also serve as a public embodiment of logical canons, however partisan the individual participants might be.

Representation, Realism, and Scepticism

In the preceding discussions I have been taking one crucial matter for granted: that the whole enterprise I have described is justifiable. But as we saw in the first chapter and later, once one begins to ask simple questions about our knowledge and its reliability, it is very easy to think it all factitious, a social construction without solid foundations. And what I have said may not seem to make it any easier to discern such solidity. Indeed, many philosophers would say that my account invites extreme scepticism, since it allows that on the one hand there is our conceptualized experience of the world and on the other there is what the world itself is like. How can we successfully make the leap across from the experience to the world it represents?

Since these questions arise naturally, and have indeed already been mentioned, I ought perhaps to say a little about how I would answer them, though this answer may not have any direct repercussions on the conduct of schooling in the way that some of the other points we have looked at probably do. The account I have offered is indeed a 'representative' theory of perception: we have experiences of what presents itself directly as a spatio-temporal world outside ourselves, but I have denied that we can simply regard the world as presented as in fact the world as it is. I have endorsed Locke's view that much of how the world appears to us is merely our contribution – whatever daffodils are like, they are not yellow-as-perceived. I have allowed that virtually all our experience comes imbued with concepts, but I deny any special authority to those concepts, and to the experiences themselves.

However we acquire the elements of experience, this account makes the fundamental question of justification the question of whether we should regard experience as revealing anything at all beyond itself. In other words, the question of scepticism about an external world. I do not pretend that such scepticism is easily answered, but I would say that once one seeks to move anywhere beyond the most attenuated interpretation of experience (for instance, filling in the gaps between blinking your eyes) then the only plausible explanatory account is the ordinary commonsensical one that there are independent objects 'out there'. It is possible to tell other stories – it is always possible to tell other stories – but none of them have the plausibility of the ordinary one.

Note that I have made explanation crucial, even at this very basic, taken-for-granted level. It is then not difficult for me to continue to insist on explanatory power with respect to the elements of the total picture presented to us by untutored perception. And so the Lockean account offered above fits smoothly into the whole strategy. That there are real daffodils out there explains our inter-mittent experiences of them; but we do not need to postulate that those real daffodils have the yellow-as-perceived that those same experiences endow them with. In both cases, what is needed for explanation is what counts.

To insist on explanatory power does not guarantee convergence on one theory of the world, but in fact at the levels and areas we have currently reached there is only one overall plausible theory, that embodied in the comparatively settled 'findings' of scientific inquiry. That is the picture technology unhesitatingly looks to.

I am thinking here of a fairly general picture of things. For reasons we shall note later, and no doubt for others too, some of the more detailed claims made in the sciences may deserve alternative interpretations. In some cases, we know that an account is only a useful picture that distorts almost as much as it reveals. It is not therefore to be taken literally. All I have claimed is that realism, the taking literally of what theories say, is the obvious line to take, the one that makes the fruitfulness of those theories intelligible.

I am also thinking of the more settled, larger-scale levels of the world. Fundamental physics operates with ideas that often seem incredible, and certainly upset the comparatively straightforward view we have at a more homely scale. While I do not pretend to understand such physical theories, what their popular interpreters say creates a problem for the view I am endorsing. There are various alternatives: we might concede that the more settled picture is in fact false on its own terms. Quantum indeterminacies may characterize everything, and the world may be a much stranger place than we imagine. Alternatively, we may allow that at the scale of microphysics things are indeed as strange as the popularizers suggest, but that the 'settled' picture remains true at a larger scale. This would presumably entail a certain incompleteness in the physical theory, but we certainly cannot rule out further developments of such theory. This possibility allows also for another scenario in which present theory is replaced by a somewhat less mysterious account, or given a less mysterious interpretation – just as we now recognize that a lot of the 'relativity' of Einstein's celebrated theories was exaggerated by early interpreters. Perhaps as much as anything else, the lesson to be learnt from the unintelligibility of popular versions of quantum mechanics is a general modesty regarding our achievements to date. Socrates, at least, would not have been surprised that we should learn how little we know about the cosmos, and indeed ourselves.

Pedagogical Relevance

We have been looking at the logical structure of our ordinary claims to knowledge of the world and of the theoretical explanations we offer of them. You might well think that by now there is not much structure left, since we have uncovered gaps all over the place. Be that as it may, the discussion so far has brought up several factors that would seem to have consequences for passing on our knowledge. Perhaps the most obvious is that all this knowledge is logically provisional. We simply cannot hope for items that will have a logical guarantee that they need never be revised. I have avoided saying much about what our concept of knowledge involves; if it does commit us to having logically unchangeable items then it is shot through with error. I don't think it does so commit us, but that may be because I am convinced of the truth of what I have said about the nature of our knowledge; I may have adjusted my concept of knowledge to fit. Some people certainly seem to think that knowledge must be final if it is the real thing. One way of taking this is fair enough: if you know some proposition then that proposition is true, and in that sense final. But our predicament is that whatever we know and whatever we know that we know could yet turn out to be false.

It cannot be denied, however, that the picture of conjectural knowledge I have presented does not sit easily with our linguistic habits. On my view we think we know a lot that we don't know. One could choose to speak differently, but any choice is likely to lead to awkwardness somewhere. Thus Bernard Williams (1985) prefers to speak of knowledge within a perspective, so that, to take an example from an earlier chapter, from one perspective we can know that daffodils are yellow and from another we can know that there is no such intrinsic property. But he then has to admit that cognitive advance can result in the loss of knowledge, which does not seem to me to be a very happy way of characterizing the situation. The general point is that the language we use has not been framed to express these sorts of truth and so it is not surprising that it does an inadequate job. That is one reason for not discussing the 'logic' of knowledge, and for recommending that you don't let yourself become preoccupied with verbal puzzles about knowledge.

It is important to note that I have been talking about logical guarantees, logical finality. The lack of this sort of logical conclusiveness does not necessarily mean that we cannot be sure, for all practical purposes, that we have got hold of some truths. I am as sure as I ever could be that I am now sitting in front of a word-processor in Mona on a fairly windy day. We are all equally certain that if we stepped out of a window on the thirtieth floor of a skyscraper we would fall to the ground rather disastrously. And of course there are a vast number of similar propositions that we all claim to know and claim to know that we know. The logical gaps we have been looking at do not require us to deny any of this. All they show is that being to all intents and purposes sure of what we believe falls short of a perfect guarantee. It is logically possible that I am suffering from some massive hallucination; it is logically possible that things will stop falling towards the centre of the earth. But these are logical possibilities that we do not regard as worth considering in our normal dealings with the world. If all our supposed knowledge were as reliable as my beliefs about where I am or our acquaintance with what happens when we drop things, making all this fuss about logical gaps would be an impertinence to would-be teachers, at least. But our knowledge isn't all like that. We may well be pretty sure about what is going on around us (in a superficial way, at least) and about some general and unspecific facts about the world we live in, such as that it has got things and people in it. But in between these particularities and extreme generalities there are a host of general beliefs about how things work and what influences what, the business of the natural sciences and human studies, which show very considerable historical divergences and where the future revision of our currently best-supported beliefs is virtually guaranteed, rather than the reverse. And it should be obvious that schools, at least at the secondary level, deal almost entirely with knowledge from this intermediate band – historical interpretations, chemical theories, biological taxonomies, etc., etc.

So in most of what we do in fact teach, the logical points are not just philosophical niceties. Rather they are reflected in the actual histories of the subjects concerned. So in those subjects, we simply cannot avoid facing the actual tentativeness of our best-supported claims to knowledge. To avoid passing on a false picture of its status, teachers should find ways of transmitting such knowledge that both concedes its impermanence and reveals why it is yet to be learnt. It is no good getting students to see only that our present views in history, science and so on are going to be superseded with the result that they think that they needn't bother to learn what those current views are. They must be brought to see also that it is only on the basis of some views that we can test others and thereby hope to make progress. They are being initiated into a social tradition of criticism which is aimed at weeding out inadequate views and testing new conjectures. Such a tradition has proven remarkably successful in some fields at coming up with views that work well enough – technology can be based on false views but successful theory-based technology suggests very strongly that the views it relies upon are at least approximations to the truth. The tradition can only do better by the students' active participation in the social dialogue of conjecture and refutation.

Teachers should therefore convey a feeling for theoretical

impermanence, and for the way that provisional status can infect our reports of data. But as Freire (1978) notes, 'the impatient educator often transfers knowledge like a package while discoursing volubly on the dynamic nature of knowledge' (p. 64).

To put the issue in terms of authority, I have denied the relevance of most types of appeal to authority in evaluating claims to knowledge. What remains is a question of whether a claim explains what is to be explained and a question of how it fits logically with other claims we tentatively accept. Explanation may not be entirely a logical matter, but it involves logical relations, and the consistency of claims is totally a logical issue, so that a large component in what is authoritative regarding knowledge is logical. The authority the teacher can appeal to is then the authority of the logical 'rules of the game' – not so much the authority of facts but rather the authority of the consistency or inconsistency between one claim and another.

Evidence and Explanation

Connected with the preceding points is a very important reorientation of one's view of the relation between evidence and explanation. Most people conceive the relation as one of evidence or testimony pointing towards a conclusion; the data give one reasons for a conclusion, or for accepting a theoretical explanation. Teachers who have been taught methods of educational research may well have been reinforced in such views by the typical procedures of feeding raw data into statistical programmes and coming out with theories of a kind: factor analyses or regression equations. Some writers have recognized how distant these procedures are from the kind of cognitive growth sketched here where ideas are formulated before evidence is collected to test them, but they seem still to be voices crying in a wilderness (cf. McDonald, 1985; Mulaik, 1985).

We have seen already that data cannot entail a theory. The Popperian view we have been sketching would suggest that we adopt a different approach and consequently different intellectual strategies. Instead of hoping to argue from the data to an explanation, we should look for alternative explanations of the data. We should not expect that the data will leave us with only one conclusion (unless we can rule out all but one of the explanations we can think of) but we can ask how well different explanations account for the data. This immediately gives us an important strategy that is not encouraged by our usual view of the matter, viz. searching for alternative explanations. You offer me some evidence for a particular conclusion; we could debate how well it supports that conclusion; but it might well be salutary to note that the existence of the data is much better accounted for in some quite different way. This could save us all a great deal of futile speculation.

It is important to note the phrase 'the existence of the data' in what I have just said. Connected with our tendency to try to reason from data to a conclusion is a willingness to treat a lot of data as 'transparent'. It says in a document that John Smith married Ann Baker so we immediately assume that John Smith married Ann Baker; or a dial reads '40 amps' and so we immediately assume that it is measuring 40 amps. But in all such cases, strictly speaking our evidence is the fact that this document or machine says something. (This is the same point we noted earlier in connection with the boiling point of mercury – we put the fullest interpretation we reasonably can on our evidence.) It requires further assumptions that things are as the document or machine says they are. If we are instead looking for alternative explanations of our data it is, I think, a little easier for us to step back from the usual trusting attitude and see the fundamental thing to be explained as the fact that the document or the machine says what it says. Once that shift is made, we need not be so inclined to take the evidence at face value.

While some teachers do now try to inculcate such attitudes to historical sources or to other kinds of data, the pressures of the normal presentation of school subjects do not make it easy for them to succeed. Evidence is in fact very rarely presented for any of the claims that are made. And for the kind of reasons sketched above relating to the cumulative build-up of theories it would in very many cases be incredibly difficult to present this evidence. So as we have seen already, school science is split between extremely simplified experimentation and the more sophisticated theorizing that has to be taken simply on trust. School history likewise in many countries still spends most of its time offering 'facts' with very little leisure for the critical examination of documents or other sources.

For both, a large part of the problem is that real work in these subjects depends on a vast array of background assumptions. These have to be told to students if they are to participate properly in the enterprise, but that is going to take up too much time. So the rigged procedures of 'guided discovery' arise (see, for instance, Driver, 1975, or Atkinson and Delamont, 1976). Or history teachers tack on an unintegrated lesson about how to examine a document critically. While I do not pretend to have solutions to most pedagogical problems, it does seem to me that if we want to engage students in something approaching real work in these sorts of subject it might be better to take circumscribed topics in which they can be genuinely immersed rather than hoping to cover vast chunks of material as well as getting an inkling of real 'discovery'. Or it might be better to give up trying to include discovery (which involves an unteachable creativity) and concentrate on the other side of the enterprise: the critical testing of ideas. In many areas there is no real need for students to know most of the 'answers' if they have grasped how proposed answers are to be evaluated.

The Structure of Explanation

One of the main claims I have made is that one important motive behind our search for knowledge is to have explanations, or to be able to understand things, or to find them intelligible. It is not just a matter of data gathering. As I mentioned in passing earlier, these notions are not totally clear. People argue about how much a statistical generalization can explain anything, and there are many other problems in giving a clear account of the requirements for explanations. But for our purposes we do not need the final and complete story about explanation. There are several very important points we can see with the aid of a simplified model.

In terms of the logical distinction we met earlier, there are two main sorts of thing we might want explained: singular claims or generalizations. (As before I shall stick in this simplification to open universal generalizations.) We might want to know why Reagan was re-elected, for instance, or we might want an explanation of the fact that gold does not dissolve in water. Typically an explanation will involve some other claims of the same logical type. If you want to understand why Reagan was re-elected you will be told other singular facts about the situation at the time. If you seek understanding of the properties of gold you will be given generalizations about the particles that make up gold molecules. But in the case of singular claims it is also very common for people to invoke various generalizations as well. In our example, you may be told about how people, or people in the USA, react to certain facts, how they seek to achieve certain goals. Even if such general claims are not made explicit, it is very plausible to say that any explanation of a singular item must implicitly rely upon some such generalizations. And it is clear that a great deal is omitted from virtually all explanations, though it must be assumed to be there if the explanation is to work.

So, putting it very crudely, all explanations will involve generalizations, and explanations of singular items will also involve some other singular items. From these facts it is obvious that we will never be able to explain everything. In any explanation there will be some claims that are not explained in that explanation. We can of course always ask for another explanation, in which these things that have been taken for granted before are themselves explained. But even this process will always stop somewhere at any particular stage of our knowledge. We may be able to ask why sub-atomic particles obey the laws we think they obey, but we may not be able now to answer that question. We may be able to take some sequence of singular occurrences a long way back, but they will still be preceded by other occurrences, whose explanation we may be unable to give. This doesn't mean that we will never be able to give such explanations; I'm not saying that there is anything whose nature is such that it cannot be explained. I'm simply saying that we will never be able to explain everything all at once (cf. what we said earlier about criticizing claims to knowledge).

How Not to Complete Explanations

One common reaction to these thoughts is that while ordinary naturalistic explanations must stop somewhere religious explanations can carry on to give some more profound and final explanation. But this is a confusion. It is in the nature of explanation that we can always ask for an explanation of anything used previously as part of an explanation. So if a divine being or intention were offered as an explanation of anything, we could always ask for an explanation of that being or intention in its turn. Put otherwise, nothing is self-explanatory. It is true that some things may appear self-explanatory in that we wouldn't normally bother to ask for their explanation, but that is a matter simply of what happens to satisfy our curiosity; it doesn't reflect some intrinsic self-explanatoriness.

There is, then, a subtle but important difference between the modesty of naturalistic science and the presumption of religion. The former simply says that we can explain up to this point, but as of now we simply have to accept that these are how things work and that this was how the universe was at some earlier time; we do not currently have any explanations of why these things are as they are. The latter is willing to agree with most of this, but it tries to add that it does have a further explanation. My point is that while that further explanation might even be true there is no reason to suppose it has the finality its supporters usually pretend to. They tend to denigrate naturalistic explanation for its incompleteness, but any explanation is going to be incomplete in that manner, so we should stop hoping otherwise.

It is perhaps worth noting that our present scientific cosmology does talk about the beginning of the universe in the 'big bang'. As far as I understand this talk, it does not alter what I have said about the necessary incompleteness of explanations since any use of the equations for the big bang has to adopt certain values for their variables, and these values are not derived from any deeper theory. They are simply brute facts. In fact one way of estimating some of them is to work backwards from our present situation by asking what initial distribution would yield what we see around us. But what we see around is just what it is; it doesn't have any self-explanatoriness built into it. And of course, the equations used to work out how the big bang developed are equally non-self-explanatory. And equally obviously, most of our knowledge in other subjects stops a long way short of the beginning of the universe!

In rejecting the feasibility of religious explanations it might seem that I have overlooked one frequent feature of such explanations. They are often answers to the question 'Why?' understood, not as asking for an account of the mechanisms involved, but rather as asking for a reason, as one asks for a reason for performing a particular action. There is nothing intrinsically wrong with such questions, but it must be recognized that there is equally nothing wrong with answering by saying that there is no such reason for something. Typically such questions presuppose an agent with

58

purposes, so one pertinent answer is to deny the presupposition, just as one hopes one can do in response to questions like 'When did you stop beating your wife?' This point is relevant when there are in fact purposes around, since at some point an explanation of the existence of the purposes will be unable to retreat to some further purposes: I may boil water to make coffee, and I might want to drink coffee to quench my thirst and get my daily dose of caffeine, but at about this point explanations in terms of intentions or purposes are likely to stop.

Coincidences and Closed Systems

I have argued that putative 'deeper' explanations offered by religion cannot do what they pretend to do. There is another area in which some religions seek to offer explanations that go beyond what a scientific naturalism would accept, an area that points up some very important aspects of scientific explanation. I have kept saying that understanding typically involves simplifications. In a lot of the sciences we deliberately simplify our problems; we abstract from the enormous complexity of the real world, and consider only what would happen in some isolated system. So in thinking about how unsupported objects behave, we start by ignoring the resistance of the air and we claim that all objects fall towards the centre of the earth with a constant acceleration. Having worked out how it would be in this fictitious situation, we can then move on to complicate the story. But the basic point is that this sort of abstraction from real complexity is typical of our attempts to understand the world. What results are a set of theories about idealized, simplified situations. One important and very common idealization is that nothing interferes with the system under consideration, that is to say, we have a theory for 'closed' systems. We can now calculate the motions of the planets to a very high degree of accuracy, on the assumption that there won't be any large and hitherto undetected object interfering with them. But of course that is an assumption, and one that may well not be true.

Since so much of our knowledge concerns the workings of closed systems, it is perhaps not so surprising that we can say very little about what will actually happen in the real world, outside of our laboratories. In that real world, we encounter open systems and so Popper's remark, 'we are very far from being able to predict, even in physics, the precise results of a concrete situation' (1961, p. 139), is not so exaggerated as it may sound. (Compare this remark by two physicists on a related theoretical deficiency: 'even the simplest system undergoing vigorous convective motion cannot be given an exact mathematical description' (Velarde and Normand, 1980, p. 79), though the difficulty in describing boiling water is due to interactions rather than to outside interferences.)

People are disheartened by the inability of economists to predict what is happening, but to expect that anyone could is perhaps to ask for much too much. What then often happens is that we can explain events in terms of their place in relatively closed sequences. But when two or more such sequences converge on one event, we cannot explain the 'coincidence', however fraught with significance it might be. So, to take a mundane example, we might explain why John Smith was standing under a particular building at a particular time by reference to his intentions, beliefs, etc. We might also be able to explain why that building was struck by lightning at a particular time (or at least we know the sort of factors necessary for such an explanation). But we have no further explanation of why John Smith should have been standing underneath it at the same time as it was struck. These two aspects of the event of his death are each explicable, but the coincidence is not; it is an irrelevance from the standpoint of the comparatively closed systems of explanation. But it is obviously the coincidence that has much greater significance for us, and that we would like to have explained. Here again many religious systems would offer explanations (witchcraft, perhaps, or inscrutable providence) where naturalistic science can only refrain from the attempt.

For our present purposes, the other important aspect of this kind of case is that it reveals a basis for some of the subject divisions we find around us. It has proved fruitful to isolate some properties of things or to attend to their constituents at some particular levels. Slicing up the world in these ways has allowed us to generate powerful theoretical explanations. We also need ways of linking the levels or aspects we have found it useful to distinguish, but these linkages may be very messy. Thriving subjects occupy the slices, less fruitful speculation, and perhaps philosophy, focus on the linkages. So, for example, historical linguistics has made progress without any serious attention to the questions of the physiology and psychology of speech production that presumably somehow underlie its results; thermodynamics is carried on to a considerable extent in isolation from the statistical mechanics that we know in principle explains it (Sklar, 1976). And a whole branch of philosophy concerns the relations between mind, or our conceptualizations of mental life, and our attempts to theorize the matter in which it is manifested.

I think it is important to stress these limitations on the power of our best supported explanations. People in general expect too much. They want knowledge that is more than the provisionally best account we can give; they want 'everything to be explained'. Instead, as we have seen, our knowledge of the world is inherently tentative, and a great deal of the most interesting is clearly provisional. Our best explanations typically involve simplifications or idealizations – they cannot then predict what normally happens in the rough and tumble of ordinary life. And simply as a consequence of their logical structure, our explanations will always leave some facts and laws of working unexplained, though not in principle inexplicable. To use two metaphors that are often invoked, Neurath's ship at sea (or Putnam's fleet of ships), any part of which can be repaired but not all at once, or Popper's city built on piles in a swamp; we should remember that both circumstances are insecure and require makeshift expedients. I have said I wouldn't talk about mathematics, but it is worth saying that the picture people have of mathematics as secure and tightly bound knowledge can mislead them into expecting a similar security elsewhere. We simply don't have it and in many respects cannot achieve it.

Concluding Remarks

To sum up the pedagogical implications of this fairly lengthy survey of the nature of our knowledge, we can see that teachers should find ways of genuinely presenting its provisional status. They should seek also to acquire and pass on a reoriented conception of the relation between evidence and explanation which stresses much more the way that explanations account for data rather than thinking of data as determining explanations. Further, they must recognize the way the development of knowledge depends on assumptions or background knowledge and a backbone of logical relations that are more permanent than the provisional data and theories we employ. They must also be prepared to recognize the ways in which knowledge revises our common-sense picture of the world and so clashes with what people are otherwise brought up to believe. The enterprise of knowledge can easily lead to what Weber called the 'disenchantment' of the world, a loss of its cosiness and its apparent endorsement of our values: an issue we shall take up in the next chapter. The search for understanding reveals a lot of common sense as ideological obfuscation. Finally we have just been looking at some of the things our knowledge and our best explanations cannot do. These limitations are equally important for teachers to pass on; exaggerated expectations can lead to exaggerated disillusionment.

4

Opinion

A bundle of conjectures is not a habitable world[4]

Facts and Values

In the preceding chapter we looked at the simplest points about the structure of our knowledge. The knowledge I was primarily thinking of was that contained in the various sciences. But people are inclined to think that the sciences are somewhat specialized; most of our active knowledge relates to the more diffuse, less specialized context of our ordinary life. The sciences are, however, convenient for my purposes because the claims we make there are usually meant to be simply factual. They are attempts to say how things are, how they work, without any other ideas or attitudes impinging on them. But much of our less specialized thinking is shot through with such attitudes or opinions. We can sometimes describe the world about us in a disinterested way – we can report that the wall has been painted pale green – but most of the time our reports reflect somewhat more involvement or engagement with the issues – we might say that the wall has been painted a pleasant shade of green, or we might indicate by some other feature, intonation or gesture perhaps, how we felt about the matter.

The distinction I am alluding to is usually discussed as a distinction between facts on the one hand and values on the other. It is not very easy to find an uncontentious way of making this distinction, partly because in our linguistic practice there is no distinction: factual and evaluative matters are tightly intertwined. Another reason is that there is serious disagreement among philosophers and other people about whether there really is an important difference. There is some difference, however, and perhaps the simplest way to see what it might be is to say that factual claims try to say how things are while evaluative claims add something about how people feel about things, about how they think we should act or choose, about which directions we should go, or about how we should judge. If you think these extra things are equally factual, then you will not think that there is an *important* difference between saying 'The wall is pale green' and saying 'The wall is a beautiful shade of pale green'; but even so you can admit that the second remark adds something to the first, viz. a suggestion about how people should respond to the colour.

Talking on the one hand of pale green and on the other of a beautiful shade of green is, as I have said already, somewhat untypical. A great deal of our ordinary language is not so explicitly factual or evaluative. It incorporates both aspects. If I say that someone told a lie I am saying something descriptive about what he said, that it is not true and was known or believed by him not to be true, but I am not making a neutral report of the fact that these things were the case; I am condemning the action. The word 'lie' incorporates the two things; it has descriptive truth-conditions (if we discovered that the person honestly believed what he said, we should withdraw the claim that he lied) but it also points us towards a particular judgement, it tells us to condemn rather than acquit or applaud. And the word 'lie' is by no means unusual; rather it is typical of the vocabulary of ordinary life.

The variety of notions which are involved here is worth some brief mention. We have just been looking at concepts like *lie* here, and in a previous chapter we noticed a similar complexity in the notion of courage. There are other cases in which the factual element is somewhat closer to the surface. One important category consists of grading terms. Eggs and vegetables, as well as examination candidates, are often graded in quite detailed ways. Typically what is involved in such grading is the comparison of individuals with a standard, either another existing individual or an ideal set of features. Such comparisons are as straightforwardly factual as you can get (although it may not always be easy to make the standards explicit, and no doubt there are cases which pretend to an accuracy and factual basis which they lack) though ascribing the grade to the individual is usually taken to be also endorsing this kind of grading scheme: choose eggs by size, rather than putative taste, for instance.

A somewhat similar comparison of what exists with a standard is involved in many judgements of fairness or justice. It is a factual matter whether someone has broken the rules of a game, though whether anything should be done about it is not. Similarly, it is a factual matter whether the accepted procedures have been followed in a trial or in appointing someone to a job, though again the decision that these procedures should be followed is an evaluation. But given agreement on such matters, these questions of fairness or justice are, from within the institutions involved, purely factual issues.

In saying that factual and evaluative matters are intertwined in much of our language I am trying my best not to commit myself to any particular theory of how this is done. One popular but crude picture involves a factual core of meaning with a free-floating evaluative appendage. You can then predict that the same factual core could be joined to quite different evaluations. There are plenty of examples where such would seem to be the case, as suggested by Hobbes:

> there be other names of Government ... as *Tyranny* and *Oligarchy*: But they are not the names of other Formes of Government, but of the same Formes misliked. For they that are discontented under *Monarchy*, call it *Tyranny*; and they that are displeased with *Aristocracy*, called it *Oligarchy*: So also, they which find themselves grieved under a *Democracy*, call it *Anarchy*.
>
> ([1651] 1929, Pt 2, ch. 19; italics in original)

and see also Flew (1975, ch. 5) for pertinent discussion. But we need not assume that it is universally true. When people do want to evaluate the same factual situation in radically different ways, then we can expect them to create the words to do so. But when such diversity is not so pressing, there need be no parallel but evaluatively different concept. The main point, however, is that even here reflective analysis can uncover the two aspects that have been welded into one. We have no excuse for avoiding the philosophical examination of the factual status of evaluations simply because of the unavailability of concepts or vocabulary.

The Logical Structure of Evaluation

Evaluative claims are, then, made by sentences that usually make straightforward descriptive claims as well. The logical relations of such sentences are identical with those we have already examined. The singular claim, 'It was wrong for John to say what he believed false' is covered by but does not entail, even in company with many analogous claims, the open universal generalization, 'It is always wrong for people to say what they believe to be false.' But given that, for whatever reasons, we have accepted some such generalization, it is built into the terminology we use so that we would now more naturally say, 'It is always wrong to tell a lie.'

Just as evaluative theory (formulated as principles rather than hypotheses) is built into reports of what is going on, so the generalizations we use are equally provisional, though people are often unwilling to recognize the fact. But as in the case of our scientific knowledge, reflection on history can bring home to one just how provisional our evaluative beliefs actually are. We often pride ourselves in fact on the amount of moral progress that has been achieved; but that is to admit that what were once thought to be acceptable principles are now seen to have been inadequate. In saying that there have been many changes, I am not of course saying that every evaluative belief has changed.

Similarly our evaluative beliefs are not overwhelmingly weighted in favour of either side of the logical fence: singular judgements or general principles. Rather, in sophisticated thought at least, there is what Rawls (1972) has called a 'reflective equilibrium': judgements of individual cases qualify principles, but principles and reflection on their applications can lead us to revise judgements on particular cases. Of course, some people, blinded by false views of the status of evaluations, can think that some particular set of principles is unrevisable; but so can they think about empirical knowledge. It is, however, often more dangerous for other people when they have such views about their own evaluations.

The Factual Status of Evaluations

While I suspect that a very great deal of what we have said about the structure of knowledge can be carried over virtually unchanged into the topic of evaluations, the most important philosophical question for us to deal with is whether evaluations are themselves true or false; whether there can be evaluative knowledge. The question is, then, whether evaluations are objectively given or whether they are only subjective.

It is worth noticing that this is not the question of whether human beings agree on certain evaluations. Clearly they do, and it is even more clear that they do when we restrict ourselves to particular social groups. Equally clearly there are other evaluations on which there is not universal agreement, but the mere fact of different opinions tells us nothing. There are different opinions about a lot of straightforwardly factual matters too; people can be wrong, and everybody could be wrong about something. So agreement or lack of it tells us nothing on its own. Again, we are not dealing with the question of whether it is good for us to think that some values at least are objectively given. It is simply the question of whether that belief is true.

I have suggested that what is often known as the argument from the relativity of values is not persuasive, at least as it is usually put. People notice quite correctly that we do things one way, the Romans do them another, and conclude that therefore there is no right way to do them. But that conclusion doesn't follow. All that follows is that at least all but one of us has got it wrong. (It is logically possible that we are all right, if the objective facts are simply that we should do things our way and they should do them theirs; but most people who want objective truths here want something less arbitrary than that – they usually think that moral principles, at least, apply to people *qua* people and not to pretty arbitrary groups of people.) But notice that this common argument proceeds in the way I suggested we reorient. It moves from evidence or data – the diversity of values – to a general conclusion about the status of values. But we have seen that no such argument is deductively valid, and that it is often better to view the matter the other way round. What do we need to postulate to explain the data in a way that fits into our other explanations of other data?

If we approach the diversity of values in this way it immediately seems that the subjectivist line about their status is in a very strong position. It says people differ because there is no fact of the matter – differences are to be expected in fact. Since moral values are part of the machinery for getting people to do or accept things they might not otherwise want to do or accept, these values portray themselves as objectively given, but this is an ideological disguise. If one takes other areas of purely factual concern where there is also considerable diversity of opinion, it is usually the case that one's explanation of that diversity will itself involve some account of how the facts are: people have differed over the shape of the earth, but you will tend to explain this by reference to what visual evidence was available to them, and this explanation will involve the way light behaves and the actual shape of the earth and the relative positions of the sun and the earth, etc. You will have to say that the earth has a certain shape in explaining why people have differed over it; but in the case of values, we do not need to postulate any such correct values. Objective values are yet another hypothesis we can well do without.

The preceding argument is very crude. Its claims about the social role of morality are highly oversimplified and incomplete, but it should indicate the way a more adequate argument would be mounted. It should also show the fruitfulness of the reorientation I argued for in the previous chapter.

But if its conclusion is accepted, we must say that a very large amount of what is taught, especially in the human and social fields, is only partly knowledge, at best. A lot of history or civics or the kinds of diluted psychology that gets into the schools is not simply factual data and theorizing, but is much more a matter of transmitting socially held values. There is now an extensive industry committed to uncovering the value commitments of large chunks of the official curriculum of schools (and not just in the human and social fields), and of virtually the whole of the so-called 'hidden' curriculum. None of this aspect of schooling can be said to be the transmission of knowledge. It is merely socially entrenched opinion. The doubts that usually fester into relativistic claims about truth are to that extent fully supported. A lot of what people are brought up to think of as truth or knowledge is a fraud. It is not true for some but not for others; it is rather not true at all for anyone. As I claimed in the discussion of truth, simple truth gives one a sharp cutting edge, which is blunted by facile talk of relative truths.

Disenchantment

In these last remarks we are focusing upon a very important aspect of the 'modern' world. In most societies, and indeed in parts of our own, social arrangements are underwritten by beliefs about the nature of things. In some form or another, societies have what anthropologists call 'charter myths'. The structures of human life, and much of its petty detail, connect with grand theorizing about the cosmos. In saying that evaluative pushes and pulls are not part of the natural world at all, but only something that we misrecognize as being there, I am endorsing that disenchantment of the world which Weber saw as central to secular modernity. A central part of education, as I conceive it, is this debunking, or at least uprooting, of many of our values.

As Bourdieu and Passeron note in passing (1977, p. 12), this creates a pedagogical problem: you cannot start by teaching the cultural relativity of cultural values, although you can hope to end up by passing on this bit of anthropological wisdom. To take a related case, you must learn some language or other in order to formulate the true belief that it doesn't matter which language you learn. Similarly, you must be given some food or other while your teacher is bringing you to an awareness of the arbitrariness of food taboos. While this is so, it should not blind us to the facts that it is possible to end up with the beliefs we are discussing and that societies vary considerably in their self-awareness of these matters.

Truths of the Heart

In this brief examination of what properly should be considered merely matters of opinion rather than knowledge, I have focused on the evaluative aspects of much ordinary thinking. But there are other aspects, of considerable importance to us as people, if not central to schooling, in which it is by no means clear that we have much that can be called 'knowledge'. Much of our thinking about ourselves is, for various reasons, in this predicament.

These questions deserve extended treatment, but perhaps we can look at one or two points now. Part of our problem comes, I think, from a misapprehension of what meaning is like. Earlier I noted that we may think the meaning of what we say is a lot more precise and definite than it actually is. We are inclined, for instance, to think that talk of emotions or motives must refer to actual determinate psychological states when it is possible that we really use such language not on the basis of internal happenings, but rather as a way of unifying complex patterns of behaviour. This possibility may seem somewhat more plausible if you consider how prone to alternative interpretations are our judgements of such matters. I may judge that A loves B while you think A is indifferent to B; both of us are tying together disparate bits of behaviour; and the question may not be resolvable by reference to what A 'feels' – she may well be deceiving herself. What then is the truth of this matter?

I do not have an answer to this question; but I raise it now to suggest that one possible answer might be that really there is no more truth here than in the evaluative case we have examined. The terms we use about each other are designed for our purposes, but as we noted long ago, telling the sober truth is not a very high priority, so they may not be contributing very much to such an aim. The truth here might not be so anthropomorphic as we would like to believe.

In general I would urge you not to make too much of a common contrast between matters of fact and matters of interpretation, since what are called 'interpretations' are often only factual accounts at a higher level of abstraction or explanatory power. But in some areas of inquiry the best we may be able to achieve is to pit one interpretation against another, without hope of any rationally persuasive resolution becoming available. This situation might arise because our concepts are not really suitable for the facts in question, or are simply too indeterminate to permit more definite progress. The concepts we use to characterize each other may well exemplify these possibilities.

Another example of misrecognition of meaning occurs in the case of abilities and aptitudes. What we have in these parts of 'folk psychology' are terms that we can use to make true or false claims on the basis of observed behaviour but which carry with them ideas that seem to refer to properties hidden from view. We use them but without having any idea of what we are really talking about. Consider different cars with different gearing: one may be ideal for driving up moderate hills, another may be very awkward. We could say the first was apt for such roads, and we would know what it is about the car that makes it so. But when we talk of a person's aptitude for foreign languages we usually have no idea whatever of what it is about that person that gives him or her that aptitude. We can also engage in debates about whether one aptitude is or is not identical with another, but since the licence to talk of aptitude carries with it no knowledge of the psychological reality, these disputes are usually insoluble. We make claims that are to some extent testable and which may be useful for various purposes, but their greatest utility for us is that we can remain in ignorance of what is going on. Again, I think people tend to suppose that they must be meaning something rather more solid than this airy emptiness, but that is virtually all analysis can uncover (cf. Brandon, 1985a).

Subjectivity and Arbitrariness

What I have been talking about is the simple truth of our evaluations, or more precisely of the evaluative aspects of the evaluative claims we make. I have argued briefly that there are no such objective evaluations or prescriptions, so that our ordinary thinking is pervaded by a kind of error here. But while I think this is a significant claim to insist upon, it must not be confused with other claims that people are often inclined to make.

As I said in the first chapter, the normal conception of what is rational or sensible or appropriate for human beings is a fairly complex one. It certainly isn't exhausted by the notion of truth. So while I have argued that our evaluations are not true or false, that claim alone should not be read as saying that our evaluations are irrational or non-rational, arbitrary, pointless or gratuitous. Some of them might be all or any of these things, but the argument so far has not impugned evaluations generally in these ways. All I have said is that, in Williams' words, 'there is no moral order "out there" ' (1973, p. 29) to back up our evaluations in the way that our ordinary empirical claims to knowledge are backed up by the way the world is.

At a superficial level we can see that these other charges need not be justifiable by returning to the fact of the intertwining of factual and evaluative matters in so much of our language. Since the use of this language is partially governed by truth-conditions, we can and do carry on lengthy and perfectly rational disputes about whether or not what someone said was a lie, or whether an action was courageous or a person saintly. If we use ordinary language, we cannot escape using such vocabulary and the descriptive claims it brings with it; and there is no other language for us to use. As we have seen, our ordinary terms for grading or ranking things or people or their performances, our ordinary talk of justice and fairness in relation to rules, as well as these less specific descriptions of character or action, all crucially and centrally involve factual matters. It is partly for this reason that some apparently 'verbal' disputes are not so silly, and why it is worth protesting at some cases of the appropriation of ordinary words for technical use when evaluative aspects are treated as easily dispensable (thus one might well think Bourdieu somewhat disingenuous in claiming that his talk of 'symbolic violence' is purely descriptive (Bourdieu and Passeron, 1977, p. x) or applaud Kleinig's (1982, p. 232) complaint that behaviourists have misused the word 'punishment' in talking of unpleasant stimuli).

But while it is important to see that we cannot use all this vocabulary in any way we happen to want, it is clearly not the fundamental issue. Using the vocabulary is normally to endorse the evaluations built into it, but the deeper question is whether we should endorse those values, and here again some people want to claim that they are arbitrary. But if 'arbitrary' includes in its meaning some idea that we could equally well do things differently, then it is very difficult in many cases to see how our in-built evaluations could be radically changed. We have an extensive vocabulary that incorporates a rejection of gratuitous violence between members of a social group. There is no objective moral law that tells us that such violence is wrong and to be abhorred, but it is difficult to see how social groups could survive or reproduce themselves if such a value were not fairly generally endorsed. (Notice that I am not supposing, falsely, that we totally reject violence, but that we reject what we label 'murder', if not capital punishment or the killing involved in warfare.) Again, to take a much more rarefied example, earlier on we noted the distinction between valid and invalid deductive arguments. I briefly explained the factual basis for this contrast, but it is obvious that an evaluative assessment is tied to the normal use of the terms as well. We want our deductive arguments to be valid, not invalid. But given what the factual basis is, and what our aims in rational argument and criticism are, it is not feasible for us to switch these evaluations around. Of course, if persuasion were our aim, the distinction and its associated values might well not matter; but given a particular 'form of life', the values have precious little freedom for variation.

Of course, there are many 'forms of life' available; and to the extent that they are up for choice their values are equally to be chosen or rejected. The peculiar deep-seatedness of our moral values perhaps arises from the fact that some of them, at least, arise out of features of every 'form of life' accessible to human beings. As I argued above, the condemnation of gratuitous violence among group members is likely to be an unavoidable feature of any human existence; a passion for rational criticism is clearly pretty idiosyncratic. The values in the former case are then not arbitrary, while it must be admitted that many people have got by without endorsing the values enshrined in our conceptualization of deductive argument.

I have been trying to counter the crude argument from subjectivism to arbitrariness. In many instances there is, however, one aspect of the situation that is worth a further comment. In suggesting that certain sorts of violence would be universally condemned, I didn't state precisely which kinds, or which factors would be thought relevant to excusing such violence. To take another and somewhat clearer case, let us consider family arrangements. All human groups have institutionalized some sort of family structure in which children are expected to be brought up (although many children will in fact be brought up in different circumstances in a lot of cases). But it is equally obvious that these kinds of institution vary considerably. Various pervasive biological and social facts about human beings may provide the basis for an argument that all human groups will necessarily have some such family arrangements; but those general facts cannot guide us as to which sort of family arrangement it will be. We must have some arrangement; but we cannot say which. It is perhaps even more obvious with language. All human groups speak a language, and perhaps they wouldn't be human if they didn't; but that doesn't force any particular language upon any group. When we are faced with this sort of situation, we have an interesting sort of arbitrariness: it is arbitrary which language or family institution we have, but it is not arbitrary that we have some language or institutionalized family structure or other.

Of course, we might be able to go on to other considerations that incline us to favour some such arrangements over others, so we might want to qualify the first claim about arbitrariness; but I think the general situation is very common and gives rise to many people's belief that the way things are done is fundamentally arbitrary. They may be at least half right in thinking so. We should also acknowledge that we tend too readily to assume that our present way of satisfying the non-arbitrary demand for some arrangement or other is clearly the best that can be done.

While I have been trying to counter a too easy move from the philosophical claim about the status of our evaluations to a premature rejection of their claims upon us, it is this last point with which I think it is salutary to conclude. Subjectivism's refusal to underwrite our evaluations allows it to recognize more easily than would other views the degree to which our values cannot be given the kinds of rational support we have been looking at. Socially entrenched evaluations are often simply a disguise for brutal and exploitative power relations; they are often based on blatant falsehoods. A view that tells us that our evaluations have no more authority than the facts of our situation and our own choices give them encourages us to hope that these sorts of atavistic prejudice and disguised oppression can be rejected and replaced. A concern for the truth about these matters of opinion might well then be a liberating force, even as it proclaims that they themselves are not matters of truth or falsehood at all.

The Teacher's Stand

While a great deal more needs to be said about these matters, we have at least the outline of a position that prompts the question: what should it mean for teachers? I have argued that a tremendous amount of what is transmitted in schools is not knowledge but socially entrenched opinion; should this fact affect the way teachers handle it?

This book takes its stand within certain assumptions that make truth, accuracy, and the strength of argument central to education. So my question becomes one concerning the educator's response to the kind of points made about values and our self-image in this chapter. People who only wish to initiate children into their pre-existing societies need make no changes.

In looking at knowledge I suggested that teachers should seek not to misrepresent it, at two levels: in terms of its repudiation of common sense, and in terms of its provisional status. Another outcome of that discussion was some support for popular pressure to stress process rather than product, the strategies of critical inquiry rather than the transient results thereof – though I insisted that one cannot have the former without assuming the latter. An important feature of the processes here is that there are not really alternatives on offer: while there may not be a simply describable 'scientific method', there is a set of overlapping critical strategies applicable to any field, and there are general aims of more comprehensive understanding in terms of which inquiry can be evaluated. So while teachers here need to be careful not to mislead, they can feel reasonably confident in appealing to the 'rules of the game' as their authority for fostering the skills and understanding they teach.

When we turn to evaluative matters, things are not so straight-forward. Several writers correctly note the distinctiveness of, say, moral or aesthetic thought, and assume that no more is needed to justify initiation into it. If such distinctive thought also embodied simple truth, perhaps they would be right (the truths would be ones that obviously matter to us). But if it does not, we need, I think, at least to be able to establish its uniqueness or unavoidability. Just as there is really only one, albeit general, way to make cognitive progress, so we should need to be persuaded that there is only one way to play the 'moral' game.

But this is very far from being obvious. Even if we allow that some components of moral thought are required by any conceivably worthwhile social life, the recent discussion of arbitrariness illustrates how little can be sustained by such considerations. Using typically rooted moral considerations, and, even more, letting one's action be influenced by such thought, would seem options rather than necessities. And so by what right can teachers initiate children into them?

My point is not simply that the aim should not be to inculcate particular evaluative views (which it almost always is in 'hidden' fact if not in theory) in favour of standard evaluative ways of thinking; but rather that in these areas there are alternative ways of thinking and that one of the main alternatives is not to indulge at all in the kind of thought in question – just as one important option with respect to religious thinking is to reject it as confusion.

Choosing among alternative courses of action, choosing among virtually unlimited ways of doing things (cf. Scruton, 1980) are no doubt inescapable features of human life. We should therefore give children access to possible principles to guide such choice. But just as we should not conceal unresolved disagreements about the cognitive status of such principles as components of a moral or aesthetic system (cf. Barrow, 1981, ch. 5), so we should not ignore the dispensability of such systems themselves. We may still offer some such system because we prefer it, but let us not suppose we have any better warrant than that preference.

So whereas the teacher can make a stand on the methods of cognitive inquiry on the grounds that they are the only way to participate and contribute to the growth of knowledge, no such basis exists for insisting on any particular version of moral or aesthetic thinking. Our cultural imperialism may well be such that teachers will continue to do so, but they are going far beyond anything an appeal to simple truth could justify.

Conclusion

So do teachers care about truth? Do you? We saw that the problem is not so much with truth in the abstract but with whether the things we teach are simply true. We also saw then, and have been considering again in this chapter, the way that what we mean can in fact be a complex mixture of different elements, some perhaps simply true, others perhaps false, or perhaps not even trying to be true. So simple answers to our question are not likely to be available.

Once we distinguish truth from what our fellows accept and press the notion of comparison built into it, it is not so easy to agree that what goes on in schools has much to do with passing on the truth. We have traditions of inquiry that have met with some success, but their tentative findings are often in conflict with common sense. This conflict is not in general stressed in schooling; it is perhaps something many of us would wish to repress. Similarly, the logical status of knowledge is often misrepresented. So schools hardly succeed in general in transmitting a defensible view of the world or of our cognitive dealings with it.

Again, despite some awareness of the distinctiveness of some evaluations, the extent of their entanglement with our ordinary concepts for characterizing ourselves is not recognized. Much is taught that represents value orientations rather than simple facts.

And even when the cognitive problems of evaluations are recognized, many writers assume too readily that such ways of thinking are somehow inescapable. Once again the desirable masquerades as the inevitable.

I have suggested that educators should at least present a defensible view of the status of our knowledge and values. The views I have presented here are of course not the only ones defended by philosophers, but they indicate limits to what can be transmitted as settled. Thus one cannot correctly teach that our scientific knowledge is fixed, or our moral beliefs straightforwardly true. A concern for truth should not misdescribe the state of debate about itself.

I have indicated some possible reorientations of our thinking and teaching about evidence or testimony and what we normally think of as the conclusions based thereon. Perhaps students can be encouraged to seek more actively for plausible alternative explanations and to take a more probing attitude to data. One can see these suggestions as yet another plea for giving a greater role to disciplined imagination in our educating. They may not be any more successful than earlier calls, but they do at least have respectable philosophical support.

I have acknowledged that a concern for truth may not be altogether comfortable; it will clash with received opinion and the guardians of the status quo; it will force choices into the open. But it may thereby promote liberation as much as it spreads misgivings. Education, as its prophets understand it, has never been a particularly comfortable or comforting process. No doubt there is much else that schools should reasonably be doing, but I think one lesson of our discussions is that when they turn to education they should be prepared for conflict.

Notes

1 'Wisdom [philosophical understanding] excels wealth.' This is the motto of Hampton Grammar School. Like the mottoes of other institutions to which I have been indebted later, it testifies to the ideological significance of understanding for education, and by its doubtful Latinity perhaps also to the fragility of our grasp of the requisite knowledge.

2 This passage comes from John Donne's *Satyre: Of Religion*.

3 Consider your race:
   You were not made to live like animals,
   But to follow after virtue and knowledge.

   The original is from Dante's *Inferno*, XXVI. The words are put in the mouth of Ulysses; Dante consigned him to Hell, but did not conceal a certain sympathy for his supposed motivation.

4 Gellner (1985), p. 126.

Further Reading

No philosophy is easy. Elementary introductions to the philosophical topics touched on here are few and far between. One of the best is W. V. Quine and J. S. Ullian, *The Web of Belief* (1978). A modern, easily available classic in the theory of knowledge, and one slanted more to traditional philosophical issues, is A. J. Ayer, *The Problem of Knowledge* (1956). A much more recent discussion, full of analytical wizardry but with a broader perspective, can be found in Robert Nozick, *Philosophical Explanations* (1981). Bernard Williams, *Descartes: the Project of Pure Enquiry* (1978) has some very suggestive discussions of our cognitive predicament, with particular attention to the role of the notion of certainty.

The views adopted in the text often derive from J. L. Mackie. His most accessible work touching on knowledge is *Problems from Locke* (1976); for truth and other logical notions, *Truth, Probability, and Paradox* (1973); for the issues raised by religion, *The Miracle of Theism* (1982); and for morality, *Ethics: Inventing Right and Wrong* (1977). Karl Popper's views can best be sampled from *Conjectures and Refutations* (1969) or *Objective Knowledge* (1972); Bryan Magee, *Popper* (1973) is a simple introduction.

Philosophical writing on truth is usually very unappealing. Besides Mackie, a good starting point is an essay in A. J. Ayer, *The Concept of a Person* (1963). A detailed account, close to Mackie's but which plays down the notion of comparison, can be found in C. J. F. Williams *What is Truth?* (1976). But like most modern discussions this book is forbiddingly technical for a beginner.

I have stressed the notion of explanation. A fairly technical classic here is C. G. Hempel, *Aspects of Scientific Explanation* (1965). Kitcher has a useful article (1981) on explanation as unification. A good discussion of understanding in an educational context is provided in a long essay by R. K. Elliott, 'Education and human being' (1975).

I have also tried to note some of the social aspects of cognitive endeavour. Here J. Kleinig, *Philosophical Issues in Education*

(1982) is good; an outstanding contribution has been made by Ernest Gellner in, for instance, *The Legitimation of Belief* (1974). He has also produced a spirited example of philosophical criticism of a branch of supposed knowledge in *The Psychoanalytic Movement* (1985).

For philosophical discussion of the physical sciences, W. Newton-Smith, *The Rationality of Science* (1981), provides a guide to the philosophical scene, while R. N. Giere, *Understanding Scientific Reasoning* (1984), sets out the logical issues very clearly. I. Hacking, *Representing and Intervening* (1983) is good on observation and experimentation.

A particularly good discussion of values, sensitive to the issues touched on here, can be found in Bernard Williams, *Ethics and the Limits of Philosophy* (1985).

Educational reflections on truth and knowledge have in general little to recommend them. Much recent debate has centred around Paul Hirst's 'forms of knowledge' basis for a curriculum, conveniently available in *Knowledge and the Curriculum* (1974). Of Hirst's commentators, Robin Barrow *Common Sense and the Curriculum* (1976) has the distinction of provoking my further commentary in 'The two forms, the two attitudes, and the four kinds of awareness' (1984).

References

Atkinson, P., and Delamont, S. (1976), 'Mock-ups and cock-ups: the stage-management of guided discovery instruction', in M. Hammersley and P. Woods (eds) *The Process of Schooling* (London: Routledge & Kegan Paul), pp. 133–42.

Ayer, A. J. (1956), *The Problem of Knowledge* (Harmondsworth: Penguin).

Ayer, A. J. (1963), *The Concept of a Person, and Other Essays* (London: Macmillan).

Barrow, R. (1976), *Common Sense and the Curriculum* (London: Allen & Unwin).

Barrow, R. (1981), *The Philosophy of Schooling* (Brighton: Wheatsheaf).

Bourdieu, P., and Passeron, J.–C. (1977), *Reproduction in Education, Society and Culture*, (trans. R. Nice) (London: Sage).

Brandon, E. P. (1984), 'The two forms, the two attitudes, and the four kinds of awareness', *Educational Philosophy and Theory*, vol. 16, pp. 1–11.

Brandon, E. P. (1985a), 'Aptitude analysed', *Educational Philosophy and Theory*, vol. 17, pp. 13–18.

Brandon, E. P. (1985b), 'On what isn't learned in school', *Thinking*, vol. 5, no. 4, pp. 22–8.

Driver, R. (1975), 'The name of the game', *School Science Review*, vol. 56, pp. 800–5.

Elliott, R. K. (1975), 'Education and human being I', in S. C. Brown (ed.), *Philosophers Discuss Education* (London: Macmillan), pp. 45–72.

Feyerabend, P. K. (1975), *Against Method* (London: New Left Books).

Finnis, J. (1977), 'Scepticism, self-refutation, and the good of truth', in P. M. S. Hacker and J. Raz (eds), *Law, Morality and Society* (Oxford: Clarendon Press), pp. 247–67.

Flew, A. G. N. (1975), *Thinking about Thinking* (London: Fontana).

Freire, P. (1974), *Education for Critical Consciousness* (New York: Seabury).

Freire, P. (1978), *Pedagogy in Process: the Letters to Guinea–Bissau* (New York: Seabury).

Gellner, E. (1974), *The Legitimation of Belief* (Cambridge: Cambridge University Press).

Gellner, E. (1985), *The Psychoanalytic Movement: the Coming of Unreason* (London: Paladin).

Giere, R. N. (1984), *Understanding Scientific Reasoning* (New York: Holt Rinehart & Winston).

Hacking, I. (1983), *Representing and Intervening: Introductory Topics in the Philosophy of Science* (Cambridge: Cambridge University Press).

Haes, J. (1982), 'Conceptions of the curriculum: teachers and "truth" ', *British Journal of the Sociology of Education*, vol. 3, pp. 57–76.

Hempel, C. G. (1965), *Aspects of Scientific Explanation and other Essays in the Philosophy of Science* (New York: Free Press).

Hillery, G. A., Jr (1984), '*Gemeinschaft verstehen*: a theory of the middle range', *Social Forces*, vol. 63, pp. 307–34.

Hirst, P. H. (1974), *Knowledge and the Curriculum* (London: Routledge & Kegan Paul).

Hirst, P. H., and Peters, R. S. (1970), *The Logic of Education* (London: Routledge & Kegan Paul).

Hobbes, T. (1929), *Leviathan* [1651] (Oxford: Clarendon Press).

Hodges, W. (1977), *Logic* (Harmondsworth: Penguin).

Holton, G. (1984), 'Metaphors in science and education', in W. Taylor (ed.) *Metaphors of Education* (London: Heinemann), pp. 91–113.

Hudson, L. (1967), *Contrary Imaginations: A Psychological Study of the English Schoolboy* (Harmondsworth: Penguin).

Illich, I. (1971), *Deschooling Society* (New York: Harper & Row).

Kitcher, P. (1981), 'Explanatory unification', *Philosophy of Science*, vol. 48, pp. 507–31.

Kleinig, J. (1982), *Philosophical Issues in Education* (London: Croom Helm).

Kuhn, T. S. (1970), *The Structure of Scientific Revolutions* (Chicago: University of Chicago Press).

Lakatos, I. (1970), 'Falsification and the methodology of scientific research programmes', in I. Lakatos and A. Musgrave (eds) *Criticism and the Growth of Knowledge* (Cambridge: Cambridge University Press), pp. 91–195.

Locke, J. (1961), *An Essay Concerning Human Understanding* [1690], ed. J. W. Yolton (London: Dent).

McCloskey, M. (1983), 'Intuitive physics', *Scientific American*, vol. 248, no. 4, pp. 122–30.

McDonald, R. P. (1985), *Factor Analysis and Related Methods* (Hillsdale, NJ: Lawrence Erlbaum).

Mackie, J. L. (1973), *Truth, Probability, and Paradox* (Oxford: Clarendon Press).

Mackie, J. L. (1976), *Problems from Locke* (Oxford: Clarendon Press).

Mackie, J. L. (1977), *Ethics: Inventing Right and Wrong* (Harmondsworth: Penguin).

Mackie, J. L. (1982), *The Miracle of Theism* (Oxford: Clarendon Press).

Magee, B. (1973), *Popper* (London: Fontana).

Mill, J. S. (1886), *A System of Logic* [1843] (London: Longmans, Green).

Mulaik, S. (1985), 'Exploratory statistics and empiricism', *Philosophy of Science*, vol. 52, pp. 410–30.

Newton-Smith, W. (1981), *The Rationality of Science* (London: Routledge & Kegan Paul).

Nozick, R. (1981), *Philosophical Explanations* (Cambridge, Mass.: Harvard University Press).

Peters, R. S. (1981), *Moral Development and Moral Education* (London: Allen & Unwin).

Popper, K. R. (1959), *The Logic of Scientific Discovery* (London: Hutchinson).

Popper, K. R. (1961), *The Poverty of Historicism* (London: Routledge & Kegan Paul).

Popper, K. R. (1969), *Conjectures and Refutations: The Growth of Scientific Knowledge*, 3rd edn (London: Routledge & Kegan Paul).

Popper, K. R. (1972), *Objective Knowledge: An Evolutionary Approach* (Oxford: Clarendon Press).

Quine, W. V., and Ullian, J. S. (1978), *The Web of Belief*, 2nd edn (New York: Random House).

Rawls, J. (1972), *A Theory of Justice* (Oxford: Oxford University Press).

Renfrew, C. (1976), *Before Civilization: the Radiocarbon Revolution and Prehistoric Europe* (Harmondsworth: Penguin).

Scruton, R. (1980), *The Aesthetics of Architecture*, 2nd edn (Princeton, NJ: Princeton University Press).

Sklar, L. (1976), 'Thermodynamics, statistical mechanics and the complexity of reductions', in R. S. Cohen, C. A. Hooker, A. C. Michalos and J. W. van Evra (eds) *PSA 1974*, (*Boston Studies in the Philosophy of Science*, vol. 32) (Dordrecht: D. Reidel), pp. 15–32.

Velarde, M. G., and Normand, C. (1980), 'Convection', *Scientific American*, vol. 243, no. 1, pp. 78–93.

Waismann, F. (1953), 'Language strata', in A. G. N. Flew (ed.), *Logic and Language (Second Series)* (Oxford: Blackwell), pp. 11–31.

Williams, B. (1973), *Morality: An Introduction to Ethics* (Harmondsworth: Penguin).

Williams, B. (1978), *Descartes: the Project of Pure Enquiry* (Harmondsworth: Penguin).

Williams, B. (1985), *Ethics and the Limits of Philosophy* (London: Fontana).

Williams, C. J. F. (1976), *What is Truth?* (Cambridge: Cambridge University Press).

Index

arbitrariness, *see* values, arbitrariness of
arguments, *see* validity
Aristotle 2, 34
Atkinson, P. 56
Ayer, A. J. 79

Barrow, R. 76, 80
beliefs 2–5, 8–9, 11, 20, 22, 26, 29, 48–9,
    53
Bible, the 34
Bourdieu, P. 69, 72

certainty 19, 34, 52, 79
coincidences 60
concepts (*see also* meaning, propositions,
    sentences) 12–14, 20–1, 32, 36–9,
    49–50, 62, 70, 76
    revision of 36–9, 46, 50, 62, 76
criticism 3, 25–6, 33, 44, 46–8, 53, 56–7,
    75
curriculum (*see also* pedagogical conse-
    quences of philosophical positions)
    1–2, 4–6, 26–7, 30–1, 39, 53, 55–6,
    68
    basis for subject divisions in 60–1
    history of subjects in 4, 53

Dante Alighieri 78
definitions 13–14, 36
Delamont, S. 56
disenchantment 62, 68–9
Donne, J. 8, 78
Driver, R. 56

Eddington, A. S. 39
education 1–3, 5–6, 8, 69, 74, 76–7
Einstein, A. 51
Elliott, R. K. 79
Epicurus 29
evidence 34, 41–2, 45, 54–5, 61, 67–8, 77
experience 20–1, 30–2, 41, 49–50
explanation (*see also* understanding) 7,
    38–9, 50, 54–62, 67–8, 77
    alternative 54–5, 77

coincidences and 60
    limits on 7, 57–8, 60–2
    reasons and 58–9
    religious 57–9
    structure of 56–9, 61

Feyerabend, P. K. 48
Finnis, J. 2
Flew, A. G. N. 36, 65
Freire, P. 2, 54

Galileo Galilei 24
Gellner, E. 78, 80
generalizations 35–6, 38, 40–7, 56–7, 66
    existential 35, 41
    logical relations of 40–3, 45, 47, 66
    open or closed 35, 56, 66
    proportional or statistical 35, 41, 47
    universal 35, 40–3, 47, 56, 66
Giere, R. N. 80
Gödel, K. 17

Hacking, I. 80
Haes, J. 1, 4, 28
Hempel, C. G. 79
Hillery, G. A., Jr 16
Hirst, P. H. 2, 16, 20–1, 31, 80
Hobbes, T. 65
Hodges, W. 11–12
Holton, G. 37
Hudson, L. 44
hypotheses 39, 43–4

ideology 48, 62, 68–9, 74, 78
Illich, I. 2
interpretations, facts versus 70

Kitcher, P. 79
Kleinig, J. 72, 79
knowledge 28–62
    as a good 2
    authority with respect to 34, 39, 54,
        74–7
    foundations of 33, 49

knowledge (*cont.*)
  impersonal 33
  opinion versus (*see also* values) 4–5
  provisional 7, 42, 45, 49, 51–4, 61, 66
  real versus supposed 4–5, 9, 47
  role of assumptions or theory in 41,
    44–6, 48, 54–6, 59, 61–2
  social or public nature of 32–3, 48–9, 53
  testimony and 31–4, 55, 77
  uses of the word 'know' 29
Kuhn, T. S. 49

Lakatos, I. 46
language, *see* meaning, nouns, sentences
  alternative ways of expressing same
    idea in 12–13, 29–30
  not developed for simple truth 18, 52,
    70
  public nature of 32
Locke, J. 29, 50
logic 9, 13–14, 18, 25–7, 31, 34–5, 40–2,
    44, 48, 54, 56, 62
  deductive 14, 26–7, 42
  inductive 42–4
  possible role in schooling 26–7, 44
  relation to ordinary thought 26, 48
Lucretius 29

McCloskey, M. 37
McDonald, R. P. 54
Mackie, J. L. 15, 24–5, 79
mathematics, *a priori* nature of 31
  security of 61
  truth in 16–17
meaning (*see also* concepts, language)
  complexity of 17–19, 24, 64–5, 69–72,
    76
  definition and 13–14, 36
means-end reasoning 3, 38
Mill, J. S. 36
mistakes 6, 17–18, 22–3
Mulaik, S. 54

Neurath, O. 61
Newton, I. 24, 37
Newton-Smith, W. 80
Normand, C. 60
nouns, abstract better replaced by verbal
    phrases 10–11, 16
  meaning as naming 10
Nozick, R. 79

observation 21, 30–2, 41, 44, 46

theory-ladeness of, *see* knowledge, role
  of assumptions or theory in
opinion, *see* values

Passeron, J-C. 69, 72
pedagogical consequences of philosophical
  positions 26–7, 29, 37, 39–40, 44,
  51–6, 61–2, 74–7
perception, *see* experience
  representative theory of 49–50
Peters, R. S. 2, 16
philosophical analysis 15, 18, 65
philosophy, concern for cognitive health
  in 28–9, 80
  need for technical terms in 6–7
  role in the training of teachers 6–7
Popper, K. R. 33, 42–3, 54, 60–1, 79
predictions 26
propositions (*see also* concepts, meaning,
  sentences) 11–12, 14–16, 19, 21,
  35–6
Ptolemy 24
Putnam, H. 61

Quine, W. V. 61

rationality 2–3, 71
Rawls, J. 66
realism 49–51
relativism (*see also* truth, theories of)
  5–6, 20, 22–4, 67–9
religious belief 2, 5, 16–17, 22, 75
Renfrew, C. 46
research, educational 54
Russell, B. A. W. 39

scepticism 21, 29, 49–50
Scruton, R. 75
sentences, grammatical kinds of 4–5,
  9–12, 14, 18
  logical kinds of (*see also* generalizations,
    singular propositions) 34–5
  propositions and 11–12
  types and tokens 12
simplifications 3, 26, 36, 41, 56, 59–61
singular propositions 35, 40–6, 56–7, 66
Sklar, L. 61
Socrates 51
statements, *see* propositions
subjects, school, *see* curriculum, pedagogical consequences of philosophical positions

teaching, *see* pedagogical consequences of philosophical positions
technology 50, 53
testimony 31–4, 55, 77
testing (*see also* criticism) 26, 33, 42, 44, 46, 48, 53–4, 56
theories 13, 44–6
theory, realistic interpretation of 50
theory, role of in understanding measuring instruments 46
thinking 11, 20–1, 31–2, 48, 75
convergent versus divergent 44
thought, *see* thinking
truth 1–29
ambiguity of the word 'truth' 16
approximations to 22, 53
certainty and 19
comparison involved in 15–16, 20–1, 76
importance for educational thought 1–3, 5–6, 25–6
in mathematics 16–17
in mythology 18
kinds of 16–17, 19
knowledge and 8–9
logical form as transmitter of 26
problems with idea of 4–6, 20
proof and 19
theories of 15, 21–5
universal agreement and 19, 67, 76

uses of the word 'true' 11
validity and 14
verification and 19

Ullian, J. S. 79
understanding (*see also* explanation) 2, 37–9, 43, 56, 59, 75
hidden structure and 38–9, 43
connecting or unifying central to 2, 38

validity 14–15, 26, 72–3
values 3, 7, 63–9, 71–7
aesthetic 5, 75
arbitrariness of 69, 71–6
intertwined with descriptive meaning 7, 63–5, 71–2
logical structure of 66
moral 5, 67, 72–3, 75
subjectivity of 67–8, 71–5
Velarde, M. G. 60

Waismann, F. 16
Weber, M. 62, 69
Whewell, W. 36
Williams, B. 52, 71, 79–80
Williams, C. J. F. 79
wisdom 2

Xenophanes 46